DELAYED LEGACY

Une stèle sera dévoilée demain en mémoire de Conrad Netting dans l'Orne

Le fils du pilote et le fils du menuisier

Ce n'est pas une fable, mais une histoire. Un lien, aussi fort que celui du sang, qui unit les familles Netting et Grandin. Demain à Saint-Michel-des-Andaines, près de la Ferté-Macé (Orne), une stèle sera dévoilée en hommage à Conrad Netting, pilote américain abattu par la DCA allemande en 1944 et enterré dignement – mais secrètement – par Louis Grandin, le menuisier du village.

10 juin 1944, au matin. Le pilote américain Conrad Netting, troisième du nom, meurt dans le crash de son avion, abattu par la DCA allemande, à Saint-Michel-des-Andaines. Un garde-forestier a vu l'avion tomber. Il prévient le curé de la paroisse et Louis Grandin, le menuisier du village. Mais déjà, le kommandantur est là. En cachette, Louis Grandin fabrique un cercueil pour le pilote. À la tombée de la nuit, le corps du défunt, laissé près des restes de son avion, est enterré dignement et secrètement dans le petit cimetière de Saint-Michel-des-Andaines. « Très touchés, les habitants du village se sont relayés les jours suivants pour fleurir la tombe du soldat », raconte aujourd'hui Michel Grandin, fils du menuisier, âgé de 11 ans en 1944. Le va-et-vient fut tel, que Michel Grandin se souvient que « les Allemands, qui ignoraient qu'il s'agissait de la tombe d'un pilote américain, ont décidé de boucler le cimetière ». Le soir de l'inhumation, le menuisier avait ramassé un morceau de la carlingue de l'avion. Dessus, il avait gravé « Conrad John » : deux prénoms ? Un nom ? Il l'ignorait. C'était trop peu en tout cas, pour pouvoir identifier le pilote. Quelques mois plus tard, le corps est exhumé et transféré au cimetière de Saint-James (Manche).

Les décennies ont passé. Louis Grandin est décédé. Michel, son fils, a gardé cet épisode de sa vie

Michel Grandin et Conrad Netting IV, deux hommes et leurs familles, réunis en mémoire du courage de leurs pères.

en mémoire, sans jamais pouvoir en savoir plus.

Une fleur, un appel à la paix

Novembre 2000. Franck Towers, vétéran américain, lance un appel. « Quand je viens en Europe, le plus difficile pour moi, c'est la visite des cimetières américains [...] Bientôt, ni moi ni mes compagnons ne pourrons plus nous rendre sur les tombes des soldats restés en Europe. Seront-elles abandonnées ? [...] Si grâce à votre action vous parvenez à convaincre les Normands de venir fleurir une tombe chaque année, j'aurai le sentiment profond de rendre un dernier hommage à mes camarades tués au combat. » Un mois plus tard, Claude Lavieille fait naître l'association « Les

Fleurs de la mémoire ». Dix-huit mois après sa création, l'association compte 900 parrains qui fleurissent plus de 2 500 tombes. « Fleurir une tombe, c'est faire un appel à la paix », explique Claude Lavieille.

Les époux Grandin ont adhéré à l'association dès sa création. « Nous leur avons fait part de nos difficultés à identifier le pilote qui avait été enterré à Saint-Michel-des-Andaines », relate l'épouse de Michel Grandin. Ils sont mis en contact avec une administration américaine, qui leur communique les détails du crash et l'identité du pilote. Le document contient également une adresse, celle de Conrad Netting IV, fils du pilote, né un mois après la mort de son père. La fille des époux Grandin lui envoie un message. Trois jours après, il appelle. C'est le début d'une longue correspon-

dance. Vendredi, Conrad Netting IV sa femme et ses enfants, sont arrivés à La Ferté-Macé, où résident les époux Grandin. Une première rencontre entre les deux familles pleine d'émotion. Samedi à 15 h, une stèle offerte par la municipalité de Saint Michel-des-Andaines, sera dévoilée sur le lieu du crash. « Nous allons aussi emmener la famille se recueillir sur la tombe de Conrad Netting à Saint-James », expliquent les parrains et la fleurissent plusieurs fois dans l'année.

Stéphanie SÉJOURNÉ.

□ **Pratique.** Les Fleurs de la mémoire 23, rue des Mesnils 50 620 Saint-Jean-de-Daye, renseignements au 02 33 56 80 66.

"The son of the pilot and the son of the woodworker," reads the headline in this French newspaper article of June 2002. As the story begins of their separate quests, and of their unpredictable meeting "in memory of the courage of their fathers," readers are assured: "This is not a fable, but a true story."

DELAYED LEGACY

A Son's Search for
the Story of His Father's Death
after D-Day

CONRAD JOHN NETTING IV

Foreword by Andrew Carroll

TRINITY UNIVERSITY PRESS SAN ANTONIO

PUBLISHED BY TRINITY UNIVERSITY PRESS
San Antonio, Texas 78212

Book design by Janet Brooks
Cover design by Sarah Cooper
Cover photograph: Lt. Conrad John Netting III beside his late father's Air
Medal in a ceremony at Brooks Field, San Antonio, Texas. Photograph
from the author's collection.

ISBN-13 978-1-59534-754-1 paperback
ISBN 978-1-59534-731-2 ebook

Trinity University Press strives to produce its books using methods
and materials in an environmentally sensitive manner. We favor
working with manufacturers that practice sustainable management of
all natural resources, produce paper using recycled stock, and manage
forests with the best possible practices for people, biodiversity, and
sustainability. The press is a member of the Green Press Initiative,
a nonprofit program dedicated to supporting publishers in their
efforts to reduce their impacts on endangered forests, climate change,
and forest-dependent communities.

The paper used in this publication meets the minimum requirements of
the American National Standard for Information Sciences—Permanence
of Paper for Printed Library Materials, ANSI 39.48–1992.

CIP data on file at the Library of Congress
19 18 17 16 | 5 4 3 2 1

To my parents

CONTENTS

——————— ★ ———————

PART ONE

PART TWO

It is the same with any life. Imagine a single day struck out of it and think how different its course would have been. Pause, you who read this, and think for a moment of the long chain of iron or gold, of thorns or flowers, that would never have bound you, but for the formation of the first link on one memorable day.

– *Charles Dickens*

Foreword

Upon first reading the wartime letters of Katherine and Conrad Netting, I was thunderstruck. Theirs was a story unlike anything I had ever encountered before.

The letters themselves are extraordinary. As soon as you start reading them you are drawn into the Nettings' world. As their wartime story unfolds, tension builds as you begin to hope that Conrad survives his harrowing missions over France and returns to Katherine. His fate adds a poignancy and resonance to the larger account, and the astonishing "after-story" emphasizes how connected these World War II stories are to the present.

What makes all war letters so valuable is that they record not only the historical details of combat, but the human side of these conflicts as well. They capture the private thoughts and emotions of troops as they deal with the difficulties of being separated from their loved ones and heading into a harsh and demanding environment. Many letters reveal the resilience and compassion of women back home who quietly carried the private pain and grief for lost loved ones. In the process of editing two books on the subject, *War Letters* and *Behind the Lines*, I found that these women—like Katherine Netting—are also the ones most likely to have organized and saved America's wartime correspondence.

At the heart of this book are the letters found by Conrad John Netting IV in a footlocker packed by his mother before the end of World War II, then left untouched until her death nearly a half century later. Conrad John Netting III was only twenty-six when his plane went down over Normandy four days after the D-Day invasion. Katherine was twenty-one. They had met three years earlier, fallen in love, and married shortly before he was sent overseas. Conrad IV was born a month after his father's fatal crash.

We'll never know whether Conrad III might have returned from the war a changed person, bearing his anguish by simply not talking about his experiences and becoming distant, like his flying buddy Pat Patteeuw. Pat had five more roommates in the six months after Conrad crashed. None came back. When Conrad IV located him in 1997, Pat reported that the feeling of separateness "lasts for about sixty years. Not getting close to anybody. I don't want to be hurt anymore."

Katherine in her own way became part of the "silent generation." She had lovingly packed her late husband's letters, uniform and other effects into the footlocker, but never mentioned the contents to her son. She went on to be a loving mother, and finally remarried after her son was grown. The only real sense Conrad IV had of his mother's enduring grief came from her unexpected and uncontrollable sobbing as they visited his father's grave in France for the first time, in 1963.

Discovering the footlocker of letters and memorabilia was the first in a series of remarkable coincidences that brought Conrad IV closer to both of his parents. At the very time that he was seeking to learn more about his father, a family in France who had witnessed his father's plane crash were beginning their search for the young pilot's relatives. This incredible development, which ultimately becomes intricately woven into the larger story about the entire Netting family, reminds us that the aftershocks of World War II echo long after 1945.

For Conrad IV, they will undoubtedly reverberate for the rest of his life.

Andrew Carroll
Washington, DC

PART ONE

INTRODUCTION TO PART ONE

The families warily approached the olive-drab containers: musty footlockers closed nearly fifty years before, just after World War II, when personal effects shipped home were put away like the war's grim memories. Recently retrieved from the rafters of a leaky and mildewed storeroom, the names stenciled on the wooden panels made known their previous owners: three brothers and their brother-in-law.

It was Independence Day 1994, and the families, gathered for a reunion, had limited expectations about what might be inside those trunks. (Though they might have intriguing contents, they might also be home to 1940s-era bugs, a thought that, despite the heat, moved the proceedings to the patio.)

The former owners were dead, leaving their children to inherit these long-forgotten assets, sort out what belonged to whom, and take away whatever was worth the trouble. As they opened one, then another, video camera running, the contents were both surprising and expected. The first opened readily, revealing some typical wartime belongings of one airman, the brother-in-law: uniforms, shoes, shower clogs, a Mae West life preserver – all in tip-top condition. Had that been all the cousins found, the day would have been rewarding enough.

The contents of the next footlockers, those of the brothers, were disappointing: hangers holding the suit tape of what used to be uniforms, a malodorous Navy mattress that went quickly to the curb in hopes that the trash men would not deem it too offensive, and a set of engineer's tools, professionally crafted as would befit ownership by a Texas A&M engineer.

That left one footlocker. Enthusiasm waned, spirits melting in the San Antonio heat. But soon that heat would not matter; the last footlocker, another one belonging to the airman, was different. Only after four attempts with assorted tools did it finally yield its grip.

Instantly, the self-conscious talk, mindless jokes, and gentle ribbing stopped. No longer was this an absurd treasure hunt in the sweltering Texas heat. The locker revealed secrets long kept by the dead, secrets that would be the first links in a chain connecting a son to his father. Out of the last footlocker came a delayed legacy.

———— ✱ ————

CHAPTER ONE

Conrad III

He was twenty-four years old and restless. Processing fuel at a refinery for eventual use by mobilized war weapons was neither glamorous nor heroic. No matter. He was contributing to the war effort, making his small contribution, and, unexpectedly, getting an occupational deferment from war service.

His employer, Socony-Vacuum Oil Company, was so impressed with his understanding of the refining business that they were ready to defer him for the duration. He wrote: "I would really like to get in [the service] somewhere, but absolutely cannot until such time as Mobilgas stops flapping [Pegasus's] wings. Socony-Vacuum will not 'un-house' me." Yet most of his friends were on their way to active duty. His best friend had been in for over a year. How glorious was it to sit in a refinery office while all that happened?

Conrad John Netting III was not alone in his restlessness. The summer of 1942 was a transitional one, when nearly everyone his age was enlisting. The country was largely consumed by war, and the war-age generation was aware of, if not obsessed by it. Not surprisingly, young people went about their lives innocently enough, with no certainty as to where they might be in a month or a year or what their role would be. But daily life became restrictive. Gasoline and certain foods became scarce as resources were diverted to support the war. The gas shortage resulted in laughable speed limits on the highways – thirty-five miles an hour – that forced civilians onto trains, if they could get on. Servicemen had first rights to train travel, with civilians inconvenienced or stranded.

This tension was most evident in every eligible-age male who was considering his options: volunteer or wait for the inevitable call. Conrad wrote to his parents in October 1940, "Found out my draft number is 2835 and that the draft drawing number is 6867. I firmly believe this will exclude me for at least a year and see no reason at this time for voluntary." Later, though, he received, through his employer's efforts, a deferment, and neither voluntary nor involuntary military service would be necessary – unless he couldn't stand the sidelines.

Then a second draft drew his number. His supervisor wrote: "I cannot hire even half-way capable men and if you feel you do not want to go, we have a place for you here for the duration." Such a deferral was a luxury and left Conrad with three choices. He could accept the deferment and continue to work for the country's good from Trenton, Michigan. He could wait for his number to be called and then decide whether to invoke the ironclad deferment. Or he could volunteer. Which choice should he make?

Until December 7, 1941, most young men in America, like Conrad, expected to lead predictable lives. They were not reared to be war heroes, did not seek some greater glory, and did not, most of them, intend to see the world. Instead, they were coming out of high school or, for the older ones, college while their country was emerging from the Great Depression. Their families, meanwhile, with depleted financial resources, were dispirited after a decade of sacrifice.

Into this economic and social unease came the eligible men born between 1918 and 1926. Their parents, survivors of the Great War, instilled a loyalty and sense of duty in their children. The children, in turn, were respectful of authority, suspicious of malcontents, and supportive of their country's ideals.

The neighborhoods that developed just before the Depression nurtured this social structure. Linking families within the neighbor-hoods were wide, accommodating sidewalks, which no one owned and which were available to all – neutral ground. For those who rocked on their front porches, hoping to catch the evening breeze, sidewalks supported a promenade of neighbors out for a stroll. Sidewalks brought parents together to exchange child-rearing tips, pleasantries, and gossip. Children gathered there to play, parade, and plot. As television would eventually become the link of the 1950s, sidewalks were the connection of the 1930s.

From the neighborhood might come your playmates, friends, and, eventually, your sweetheart. While occasional movies downtown, a sports team, your church or synagogue, or visits to relatives might open opportunities beyond, these sources were secondary and would rarely provide more than an acquaintance or two.

This social pattern fostered in young people a loyalty to neighbors and a respect for elders that was deeper than they could learn in a classroom. They learned it, too, from their parents. The children, in supportive neighborhood clans, grew up with little rebellion. And those children of the 1930s brought, in the early 1940s, this loyalty and respect to their military units – which around the world doubled as surrogate neighborhoods.

* * *

The Netting family, immigrants in 1880, easily settled into the social structure of the American neighborhood. Johann Konrad Netting (the family surname was originally Swiss, *Nöthing*, and meant "neat person," a description that would be dead-on for successive generations) and his family left Germany for a new life in the United States. His son, Conrad John Netting, apparently precocious for his age, convinced his father to move.

In 1963, Johann's grandson, Conrad John Netting Jr., wrote: "Kaiser Wilhelm was Emperor of Germany and demanded that every youth-male must join the Army. My father did not approve of such regimentation. Therefore, he persuaded his father to go to America. He was ten years old when they left Germany and came across in steerage" on the *SS Rhynland I*, Red Star-American Line.

Pontiac, Michigan, the family felt, held promise, as it was a receiving point for other immigrants from Germany. From the diary of Conrad Jr.: "My father entered school but could not speak the language and thus school had little interest for him. He went as far as the seventh grade and decided he would go to work." He worked on a farm throughout his teenage years. Seeing no future in the backbreaking work of a farmhand, he moved in 1888 to Detroit. In 1891, he married another recent immigrant, Clara Beckbessinger, in a match arranged by their parents. They would have four children, one of whom would later be elected mayor of Grosse Pointe, Michigan.

Conrad Sr. worked for a chandelier company, learning the business at the lowest level and substituting chutzpah for a formal education. By age thirty-seven, he was president of the company and its Canadian affiliate. As gas fixtures flickered and electric ones began to command the market, he foresaw the trend and began to supply the more desirable fixtures to Detroit's swelling population. His niche, conveyed in the slogan "fixtures for the better homes of Detroit," helped him find quick favor with established families and their businesses.

Eventually this included a friendship with Henry Ford. Conrad Sr. was one of the business people Henry Ford approached in the early 1900s to become a stockholder in the newly established Ford Motor Company. Though he apparently never did buy stock, Conrad Sr. remained friends with Mr. Ford, who gave him the following handwritten note: "Please [allow to] pass Mr. C. J. Netting and friends anytime and anyplace. Henry Ford. December 28, 1914."

After solidifying his business résumé, Conrad Sr. became active in political circles and in Christian causes. He wrote to one of his sons, Ralph, in 1917: "Had a pleasant experience with the new governor [of Michigan]. The Governor . . . motioned for me to come to him, bid me to sit down on the other side of his desk and let the politicians wait while we had a nice little chat. The state legislature this year seems to be above the average and I believe that they will refrain from enacting too many laws, one great trouble with most all legislatures or congresses included."

The Nettings were devout Christians, members of the First German Baptist Church. Conrad Sr. found time for two terms as president of the Detroit Baptist Union, and four terms as a member of the Michigan Legislature. *The Detroit News* reported in 1933: "While acting as foreman of a jury in the Federal Court, [Conrad Sr.] startled his fellow jurymen by suggesting that they begin their deliberations with a prayer. They liked it, also, once they had tried it."

Unlike his father, Conrad Jr. would complete high school. Just before his graduation in 1911, his high school teacher dispatched him into the larger world with an inspiring valedictory.

Your future life will depend much on your cares in school, which I am sure you have so manly mastered, and by steady industry, [and] care of that health with which

God has happily blessed you. You may hope to ripen into a respectable and useful member of society, and to render yourself fit to encounter those responsibilities, which fall to every man's lot.

We are all of us too apt amidst the bustle and enterprise of everyday life, to forget Him upon whom our very life utterly depends, and to think only of worldly success, while we lose all thought of the life for which our present existence should be but a preparation.

Let me express a hope, my dear Conrad, that you will think goodness preferable to greatness; that you will study the cultivation of the soul as well as of the mere intellect; that you will recollect how great a virtue is reliance on God, and how noble self-reliance is the result of such virtue.

Clara Netting was not shy about advising her son. In his childhood bible is an admonition written for him: "Search the scriptures for they are a Lamp to your feet, and a Light to your path, and lead to Eternal Life."

The C. J. Netting Co., "purveyors of fine chandeliers for Detroit," expanded its business significantly. Indeed, the 1920s would encourage any business that catered to those who were making their fortunes on the automobiles rolling off the production lines, and on the stock of such companies. In 1923, seeing another opportunity, Conrad Sr. founded the C. J. Netting Land Co. to capitalize on Detroit's population growth. His home on Pennsylvania Avenue, in one of Detroit's more desirable neighborhoods, validated his rise from illiterate immigrant to prosperous citizen.

Conrad Jr., now secretary-treasurer of his father's prosperous company, married Rosalind Bishop of Detroit in March 1917. Into the close, multi-generational Netting family was born the first grandchild, Conrad III, on June 7, 1918. A second child, Robert Wesley, was born in 1920.

Conrad Sr. was now over fifty years old. With capable hands running his businesses, he and Clara took their winters in Florida. He continued to offer business advice to his son, in whom he had abundant confidence. As Conrad Jr. made the business his own, his father wrote him in 1923: "It is my hope and prayer that God may give you strength, health and wisdom to prove that [my] confidence has not been misplaced. Let no day go by, but that you will ask our Heavenly Father to guide you and you will be surprised by the help He will give you, solving problems at difficult times and above all being just and at the same time merciful."

Although every element of the family's life seemed to be in harmony, the stock market crash of 1929 and the ensuing Great Depression devastated their businesses and, ultimately, their financial reserves. Customers who were buying the best and brightest in the 1920s hunkered down in the early 1930s. The Netting businesses and self-made fortune were lost. Conrad Jr., now without a job, broke away from the security of Detroit to seek a new path.

By today's standards, a road trip in September 1933 could not have been much fun. Throw in two boys, ages fifteen and eleven, and the scene hardens. Yet it must have appealed to Conrad Jr. and Rosalind, for off they went, leaving behind parents and siblings, social standing, a business infrastructure that could have launched a new career, and political connections.

Twenty years later Conrad Jr. wrote that his inspiration to head to Texas came from a quotation about the early wagon trains that took settlers out West: "The cowards never started, and the weak died along the way." If this compelling expression was the Nettings' sole impetus for pulling up stakes, then two generations later it seems inadequate. What else might have caused them to start over?

No evidence exists to support the claim, but Conrad Jr. may have been looking for the opportunity to do something on his own, to demonstrate that he could succeed without the social scaffolding erected by his father. In his later life he had little connection with Detroit. One relative said, "He stood alone so well." This yearning for independence from a strong father figure – and from social regimentation – would repeat itself in the next generation.

Conrad Sr., supportive of his son's fresh start, wrote in 1933: "Put up a real fight against the adverse economic conditions prevailing at the present time. Only he who endures is entitled to the fruits of Victory."

Strong Teutonic organizational skills were not lost on Conrad Jr. After a thorough analysis of available opportunities, he settled on the Rio Grande Valley in South Texas as the region with the most chance for surviving the Depression. He had visited the area in about 1913 and saw its potential. Now, with a family to support and little income, he started his own business, as his father had before him. He sold packaged orange juice made from the thin-skinned, juice-laden oranges that grew in the fifty miles of fertile fields from McAllen to Brownsville.

Within two years, however, the family uprooted to San Antonio, bringing the Netting Food Products business with them. Conrad Jr. felt "San Antonio had the best possibilities of any region in the country."

The San Antonio Nettings seemed to be on their way to replicating what the Detroit Nettings had done a generation earlier. Conrad Jr. and Rosalind had a love reflective of what they had seen between Conrad Sr. and Clara. Conrad Jr. adored Rosalind and was wholly devoted to her. One relative said: "I saw him express total and unfailing love to her. . . . He saw . . . his family in a glass brightly. We were perfect to him. If we had any momentary problems, they were nothing but opportunities for us to express our superior ability to handle them."

He and Rosalind owned their fledging food products business and would enjoy the independence, and suffer the sacrifices, it would bring. Conrad Jr. quickly integrated himself into San Antonio's business community; within weeks of his arrival he was a member of the San Antonio Rotary Club. Building on their Christian faith, the Nettings joined St. Mark's Episcopal Church, where their boys would fill several church roles as befitted young men, including service as acolytes.

Conrad III and Bob, supported by the Netting family in both Detroit and San Antonio, led typical lives of 1930s teenagers and by most accounts were sensitive and appreciative sons. They attended Jefferson High School with friends from their neighborhood. Conrad's high school activities included the lead in the senior play and the literary editorship of a quarterly magazine. Though the school had a significant R.O.T.C. program, Conrad was not involved, an early indicator of his distaste for regimentation, wholly consistent with that of his grandfather.

✳ ✳ ✳

Friendships begun in high school often survive for lifetimes. The experiences and transitions affect youths in ways that those in later life do not. Even though he was in his San Antonio neighborhood for only three years, Conrad III found the friend of a lifetime. Randall Henderson and he were the perfect match. Similar in height, under 5'10", and in appearance – easy walks, open demeanor, rimless glasses – the boys were broad shouldered and almost thin. Their birthdays were just eight months apart, enough distance to put Conrad one year ahead of Randall in school. Without knowing it, Randall and Conrad were forging an interdependent link that would merge their families and survive even death.

Both were engineer material, so they packed off to the Agricultural & Mechanical College of Texas, better known today as Texas A&M University. Building on the strong religious faith held by his parents

and grandparents, Conrad at once sought the rector of the Episcopal church. He wrote his parents in September 1936: "I had a talk with the Episcopal rector tonight. They have communion the first Sunday so I'll get to go there." He and Randall roomed together.

Texas A&M, even in the 1930s, could muster a loyalty that it is not easily understood by non-Aggies. The A&M traditions, with their military underpinnings, instilled an enthusiasm and devotion still admired

Conrad John Netting III when he entered Texas A&M University in 1936.

by other schools. Students' loyalty to the campus and its culture, traditions, and folklore is legendary.

Conrad arrived at Texas A&M ready to conquer the school, the classes, and the system. But doing so wouldn't be any fun without friends. He and Ross Novelli were thrown together their freshman year and quickly became friends. Ross recalls the A&M dating and party system: "[T]here were two pretty girls [twins] in Marlin, Texas, and Connie and a friend would hitchhike over for dates. In those days, we called the decent dates the Bryan [Texas] 400 who only dated the [boot-wearing] Seniors. And so, some of us had to travel for a date. . . . [Later,] I remember Connie being with us while we were all drinking beer from a quarter-keg (we had Southern Select Brewery then) and telling stories at the [fishing] camp."

But Conrad's nature, apparently dominated in educational matters by his grandfather, worked against him. First, he was adverse to regimentation, and at Texas A&M everyone and everything was regimented. Second, he was not meant to be a student. Borderline grades and an itch to work ended his college career, just as they had ended his grandfather's middle school career.

The rewards of a college degree must have been evident to Conrad. If he sought to be an engineer, he would have meager career and salary prospects without a diploma. His parents must have been adamant that he continue in school and bring up his grades; no doubt the money they allocated for his education was a large percentage of their resources, and, with another son to educate, those resources were limited. By this time, however, Conrad Sr. had gone back into business, at age sixty-three, and made another fortune, thus assuring possible support from Detroit.

The decision to stay in college must have been distracting, and the resulting tension considerable. Though Conrad should have stayed, he didn't. His father wrote, "Conrad continued at A&M for two years but he found practical experiences far more interesting so he [worked for] Magnolia Oil [in Trenton, Michigan] as a permanent employee."

Conrad's feelings during his return to Michigan in 1938 are undocumented. Why Michigan, unless his grandfather had brokered a job for him? Why drive so far unless his other opportunities were slim? Was this an escape from one autocratic relative to another? In fact, Conrad III's supervisor had been a friend of Conrad Sr. for many years, suggesting that he brokered the job for his grandson.

Strong personalities are the long suit of the Netting males. Conrad Jr. may have left Detroit to escape his father's overbearing attention. Now Conrad III might be leaving San Antonio for the same reason. He wrote: "It's about Dad and me. We always have been at terrific cross odds with each other and we've never even half way gotten along with each other. I love him with all my heart, naturally. But we're always fighting." Decades later a relative confirmed: "[Conrad III] informed me he did not think he could ever live happily in the same city with [his father]. [Conrad III] viewed him as an overbearing man, autocratic, willful, demanding." But remember that this is a son of about twenty and a father of about fifty, so such tension could be a product of the then unheard of generation gap.

Sebastian Faulks, in his World War II novel *Charlotte Gray,* wrote:

> *The love of a man for his son is a terrible and wonderful thing, one of the greatest that God has given to us. It is comparable to the love of God for man. This of Abraham, prepared to kill his long-awaited son Isaac, to plunge his knife into the living boy. God chose that test because it was the hardest. And to save the world he gave his own Son.*
>
> *In what a father feels for his son, there is much stern hope, but so much tenderness that I cannot describe it to you now. If you have sons of your own you must hold them when they're young. But you will never keep them in that embrace. They are separate from you, however much you love them, and all you have done, in a moment's passion, is create the circumstances for their existence.*

With time to ruminate during the trip, Conrad probably was floundering. His best friend was still at Texas A&M, his buddies were in San Antonio or would return there, and here he was, 1,500 miles away, without prospects for a college degree or much of a future.

* * *

Four years later he faced, in the spring of 1942, a decision of even more significance. Should he volunteer for the military, wait to be called, or use his good-as-gold deferment? On such decisions is character made. If he chose the service, he would be more actively and noticeably serving his country. He'd have that in common with his friends. But with America's involvement only six months along, no doubt years would pass before the war was over. Could he surrender those years?

As a war-critical employee, his life did have its moments. With fewer men around, the young ladies of Michigan were short of dates, and Conrad Netting was a desirable escort. But his scorn for society's trappings meant he would not be climbing any social ladders with Detroit's most eligible young ladies. So, although this young man was handed a Detroit-based social life on a silver tray, he spurned it.

Movies, sailing, dinners, and occasional bar hopping provided the young set around Trenton with plenty to do, though little fuel (despite Conrad's connections) or excess funds to do it with. One way to cut costs was to stay home. Conrad wrote: "This apartment has a grand recreation room and bar and . . . it would be foolish not to cash in on same and have an occasional party. They are parties long to be remembered. In fact, no one has yet forgotten any of them." Later a friend wrote: "His nickname was 'Party Boy.' He loved to have a party; he loved to go to a party." Though he lived in San Antonio for only a few years, he was inclined toward Mexican food dinners, which he called "sacred food." Not much of that in northern Michigan.

"I am dating (still) Verna – a beauty, probably in love with a soldier somewhere," he wrote on May 12, 1942. "I'm dating Betty" was in the follow-up letter on June 1. And, of course, to whom was he writing all this probably unrequested information about the women in his life? Yet another young lady, Katherine Henderson, sister of his best friend, Randall. But she was in San Antonio. With all the restrictions and rationing, writing was his sole means of contact. She was only a ten-cent airmail stamp away.

Conrad's carefree party life would not sustain him indefinitely. He didn't feel right about the direction his life was heading, and with good reason. Though he didn't know it, he was entering an exceptional time. Along with his peers, he was going to help write history.

CHAPTER TWO

———— ★ ————

Katherine

As with most high school classes, the class of 1940 felt unique and unhurried. In time the seniors could pick from the choices that lay before them. College for those who could afford it, and careers, marriage, and children were theirs for the picking. And what was the rush? In the summer of 1940 they could wait and see, take their time, let events unfold.

Eighteen months later all that was a memory. After Pearl Harbor and the whiplash it created, it was time to check the choices, make decisions, and opt for the best fit in a life turned upside down.

While the young men, boys really, were making military decisions that winter – enlist, volunteer, wait – the girls had their own agenda, largely instinctual. The boys were leaving, and if the girls weren't in love quickly, when would they get their next chance? Their parents were talking about "the duration," and though they might not know exactly what that meant, it sounded like a long, long time.

The wait-and-see of 1940 would become the time's-a-wastin' of 1942.

For many girls, those mere eighteen months had been put to good use. College might be well under way, for instance. But for those without means, or with brothers who surely needed a college education more than they did, a clerical job was the answer. This both added to the household income and helped a young lady feel she was contributing to her room and board at home.

And what about home? Inevitably, it was still Mama and Daddy's home, with maybe some siblings thrown in and a grandparent too. Several generations commonly lived together to scratch their way out of the Depression.

This was the world of Katherine Henderson. Just seventeen years old that winter, she could have been the poster girl for the 1940 high school graduate. Smart, popular, resourceful, cute, and pretty (she had the looks and personality of Katharine Hepburn), she had every intangible gift. Unfortunately, she had few tangible ones, as her family's finances had suffered mightily during the 1930s.

Her three older brothers could defend her from adversaries or tease her just for being a kid sister, and jump instantly between the two. If she faltered at a project, they would say, as lovingly as possible, that she had acted stupidly. When her high school girlfriends heard this, Katherine put her resourcefulness in high gear and co-opted the nickname Stoop. Not a bad win for her side.

That was kid stuff. Now she and her peers were confronted with life-changing decisions. Not as forward-looking as she, her friends scrambled to warm up their decision-making machines. Should a boyfriend be military bound, a hurried wedding would assure love and letters from across the oceans.

Katherine was more practical. She wouldn't go chasing some dream only to catch a nightmare. She wouldn't rush her decisions. Time was her friend.

* * *

Any child, especially a girl with three older brothers, one thirteen years older, had better be resourceful and maintain an overload of self-esteem. And if you weren't born with it, you had better figure out how to get it.

Katherine's lineage, from both the Hendersons and the Millers, reached back to pre–Civil War Georgia. Before that war ended, her great-grandmother left Georgia and headed for Galveston with a trunk full of Confederate money. Within a short time, its best use would be wallpaper. Still, the family's gracious and accommodating southern style brought them into contact with many of Galveston's finest families at a time when Galveston was on a par with New Orleans and Charleston for cultured living.

All that changed when the 1900 hurricane nearly destroyed the town. What wasn't destroyed was breached so badly that Galveston never recovered. Tiring of Galveston's susceptibility to hurricanes, the family moved inland to San Antonio. Katherine was born in 1923.

Katherine's father, Francis Tennille Henderson, settled on a career with Gulf Oil Corporation that would last for twenty-nine years. The job required him to be in Mexico for nearly all of those years, leaving his wife, Maud, to maintain the household and raise four children (a fifth died in 1918 at the age of two). Katherine wrote many years later: "I resent the fact that my father never lived with me. Probably a psychiatrist would describe this as a rejection complex." Her father died in 1953, having maintained his separate life in a foreign country with only minimal contact with his family.

The family home held three generations, including Maud's mother, in its meager rooms: a parlor, dining room, three bedrooms (though one was merely a sleeping porch), and a kitchen the size of a large closet. Privacy for a young girl must have been a challenge, though Katherine took it in stride.

Her teen-age life revolved around her friends, many of whom were neighbors or attended school with her, or both. By the time they graduated from high school, they were inseparable and would remain friends until their deaths. Who else but your fiercest friends could you call nicknames that rivaled Stoop – names like Greasy, Scratchie, Dodo, Ace, Cupcake, Piggy, and DeeDee?

Carefree to a fault, the girls dated, gossiped, wrote silly letters, and played dominoes occasionally and bridge endlessly. Katherine dated often, but at just under 5' 8", she was taller than many boys. Her personality carried her through many uncomfortable evenings. She harbored no grudges, found no boy unacceptable (no matter his height), and could buzz around with any girl from her class. More than one called her a beloved friend.

During those years, her brother Randall, five years older, would come home from Texas A&M and bring his best

Katherine Henderson in 1942, about the time of her first date with Conrad III.

friend with him. Though this friend lived a few blocks away, he spent an unusual amount of time at the Hendersons'. Randall saw Conrad's visits for what they surely were – a chance to keep eyes on his younger sister. But Conrad was too old to date a high school girl, so casual meals and chance meetings were the extent of their contact, all under Maud's watchful eye.

* * *

In 1940, as Katherine left Jefferson High School, the most beautiful school in the nation according to *Life* magazine, she had time on her hands.

Two of her older brothers, Tennille Jr. and Randall, had graduated from college, and the third, Jimmie, went straight into business. Money for college must have been short to nonexistent. Still, Katherine enrolled in the local community college, taking core courses and commuting from home. Though Randall and Conrad wrote often, in April 1941 Randall received an unusual letter.

> *Do you know something? I got to thinking about something that perhaps I have no business thinking about. But, please bear with me while I at least make an attempt to state my case [for] Katherine. I cannot imagine now why I didn't follow the dictates of my heart & mind . . . and ask her for a date. The fact is, I'm kicking myself for not having that date with your sister. Wonder what I could expect should I write her? Never mind, I was just wondering.*

Conrad was in Michigan by 1940; Randall left for the war in the summer of 1941. Other than occasional visits home, which were difficult to manage, Katherine and Conrad couldn't have been together before 1941 for more than a total of a few hours. Yet here he was discreetly asking Randall for permission to date his sister. Randall must have cooperated, for on April 23 Conrad wrote his first letter to Katherine.

> *Dear Katherine:*
> *This is a letter to [Randall's] sister, Katherine. She has long been my favorite of all favorite secret loves. With*

this in mind, & remembering that a secret love can hardly remain secret when such love becomes known, I send you greetings from the north, the frigid north.

May the blessings you so richly deserve eternally be yours, & may you never fall from the pedestal you so graciously adorn.

Your admirer, Conrad III

For the next several months the letters continued. By January 1942, Katherine was fantasizing about marrying him. She wrote in one girlish note to a friend that she would, "after twelve years of married life with Conrad J. Netting III, have four or more children (preferably boys)."

By now the war was daily news. Boys were volunteering in droves, leaving within weeks. Katherine felt, of course, that she was immune from the timing problems of courtship, marriage, and kids. Her fantasy bridegroom had been deferred from service.

★

CHAPTER THREE

Courtship and Change, 1942

Was there a life in America that wasn't altered by Pearl Harbor? The old issues now looked comical in their shallowness. Thoughts of sports, new cars, spring planting, fashions, and the Great Depression were yesterday's news. Instead, people discussed Midway, a place no one could have found without a magnifying glass a month before. They talked about rationing and how meat, tires, stockings, cars, and gasoline were now bought with coupons, if at all. The war was Topic One. No two people could meet without ruminating on the latest friend to be sent overseas. Americans' lives had gone from orderly and methodical to utter confusion, like an ant bed after a kick to its middle.

Men filled the Mobilgas office in Trenton and would have gathered at the cooler to discuss the headlines or a family's latest contribution to the effort. Though many were above the draft age, others had to wonder if their work was good enough or important enough for "occupational deferment," the magic words that would keep a man at his desk for the duration. Some, eager to be involved, had already left. Others stayed, feeling they could contribute more with brains at the office. Wasn't it true, as the poet John Milton put it, that "they also serve who only stand and wait?"

There never was a time in American life when so many people were involved in a shared cause. It was a time, as Tom Brokaw put it, of "conspicuous patriotism." If your contribution was at a desk, it was a hard sell to your friends to suggest you could do as well there as overseas. Many did serve that way, and just as heroically as those facing the enemy.

As he wrestled with where his patriotism could be used best, Conrad took counsel. He wrote in May 1942: "Randall wants me to get in the Air Corps and I'm thinking seriously of doing it – as an aviation cadet first, at $75/month, then a commission in the said Air

Corps. It would be ground crew, armament division or something similar." By this time his best friend had been in the Air Corps almost a year and was voting for Conrad's active service, not desk duty.

That May, before Midway, talk would have been about how poorly the war was going. Singapore had surrendered, resistance was futile in the Philippines, and Japan's stepping stones to Hawaii were obvious. Japan could pick any reasonable course to take the war: Hawaii, Alaska, and the U.S. west coast were viable options. Would a young man consider his meager contribution too little, too late? Was negotiated peace not on the horizon?

Guidance probably came from Conrad's parents. By now Conrad Jr. had changed careers twice, then signed on with civil service, moving with Rosalind in 1941, at age fifty, to Dallas. There he was assigned to the Army Corps of Engineers. His commitment to the nation's service must have spoken volumes to Conrad III. As his father applied his intellect to the problems of the war, so might he have advised his son. But in 1942, few parents urged their sons to battle when an honorable deferment was in hand. And the Nettings' other son, Bob, was at Annapolis and destined for a career in the Navy. Did one family need both sons in the war?

Conrad could weigh his decision in a vacuum. Other than his parents and his brother, he probably believed his decision would closely affect no one else. He could take risks. He could face death, even, and its ripple effect would stop with those three people. In 1937 he wrote, "Death has to come some time or other, so all we can hope to do is make the most of our lives in the time provided." Did he still believe this five years later?

* * *

Complicating matters were his letters to Katherine. With his parents now in Dallas, he had no link to San Antonio other than Randall. Needing to call someplace home, he listed Randall's address on his official records. This meant that Katherine lived at Conrad's permanent address, an issue to consider in those less liberated times. But living with his father would have been difficult. In 1942 he wrote: "Strange, isn't it, how Dad and I have such a helluva time getting along with each other and yet we're simply devoted to each other. And then – Grandpa. I'm crazy as all get out about him. Always have been, always have admired him, have always been able to work smoothly with him – because he gave me credit for being twenty-one years old. Something Dad still can't realize." This father-son relationship appears normal then as now.

And what about Katherine? He'd had eyes for this girl when she was only in high school. Now she had matured into a nineteen-year-old with college credits and a job with the base engineer at Fort Sam Houston in San Antonio. No evidence exists, but their romance must have blossomed while Conrad was away. In early 1942, Katherine was daydreaming of marrying him and having four boys, though he likely was unaware of this. In April, in a first letter to her, he wrote, "Seriously, Katherine, I have wondered how you have been getting along – whether you are still holding out for *the* fellow, or whether you are waiting for me."

Katherine, ever the optimist, must have felt as though her life were on track. Conrad had confirmed his interest in her, and she knew of his deferment and that he had selected her home as his. She could assume that his inclination was to settle in San Antonio. All these factors pointed toward the life she and her girlfriends dreamed about. Given time, wouldn't it all work out?

Then, barely a month after their first letter, Conrad wrote:

> I have definitely made up my mind to get into this mess and seek out some action somewhere. The less said of the "why" of all this the better. Briefly, and to the point, it is this. (1.) Inaction here is driving me nuts. (2.) All my friends are doing something. Some have already seen their [draft] number come up. (3.) It is well worth while not for my own interests, but for the good I feel I can do. So, with [three] letters of recommendation I made application as an Aviation Cadet in the Army Air Corps. I would like to get out of here and get somewhere where something is doing, and I won't rest until I do.
>
> I feel this way about it: true, I had a pretty good job in an industry that is without question vital in regard to

the war effort. But why should it be that a brat like me should be desking himself through this business when I am qualified to get into active duty somewhere. And that is that.

This urge to serve, to do better and be better, was not unique to Conrad or his generation. Ralph Waldo Emerson caught the essence of it in "Voluntaries."

So near is grandeur to our dust,
So near is God to man,
When Duty whispers low, Thou must,
The youth replies, I can.

Katherine must have been a wreck. Her timetable was in shambles, her future upside down, and the man she loved – it was love, wasn't it? – might be taken away from her. But what a man to turn your life inside out! Who could argue with his reasoning: "My greatest admiration: the once-free peoples of this earth, who, in spite of all the intolerance they have had to bear, fight on. To them, I sincerely and reverently, doff my hat. To them goes my heart."

Between the decision to "get into this mess" and being accepted into it were several obstacles. Probably on Randall's recommendation, Conrad selected the Army Air Corps. Randall's poor eyesight kept him from flying. Maybe to one-up his friend, Conrad picked flying and, given the choice, piloting. He made up his mind in June 1942 to fly, but as pilot, bombardier, or navigator depending on the test results.

One criterion was a physical, which had a stringent vision requirement of 20/20 for pilots. Conrad knew before the physical that this was going to be tough. His vision was 20/20–4, which might make the cut depending on how relaxed the examining officer was. He wrote to Katherine: "The Major and I are a cinch to go round and round [about] my 20/20–4 vision. I have been informed that this is the minimum, but they are holding up my appointment because of it. Feel that on reexamination I could pass." Within a month he wrote: "I'm in it – officially. Subject to the twenty-four hr. call, but we were told it would probably take about sixty days."

Katherine had her options. She could walk away, forget the whole silly mess, and wait for someone else. That, of course, was problematic since eligible young men were streaming to their ports of call. Or she could make the best of it. Conrad was, after all, something special. Besides, just because he was "in it – officially" didn't mean he would leave her, go overseas, be hurt, or worse. Too much had to fall apart first. All he had done was volunteer; Katherine was probably unaware that Army Air Corps pilots had a higher-than-average mortality rate. If she supported his decision, she would have to adjust her thinking, get on his side without revealing her misgivings. To do so, she might have considered one of her favorite poems, "Outwitted," by Edwin Markham:

> He drew a circle that shut me out –
> Heretic, rebel, a thing to flout.
> But Love and I had the wit to win.
> We drew a circle and took him in.

Draw the circle she did. "Con," she wrote, "please hurry home and I mean to Texas and marry up with me."

By that summer, Conrad had been in Michigan for over two years. Opportunities for social contact with Katherine had been at best infrequent. Their first date would not be until October. Yet here they were, talking of marriage and children. "Those lads of ours are going to be Episcopalians," Conrad wrote. This was the exact position Katherine had vowed to avoid. An impetuous courtship, a hasty marriage, and, if events developed, a too-quick pregnancy were not how she had planned her life.

Before this talk of marriage went any further, they had to get to know each other better. And if they couldn't date, their letters would carry the load.

Conrad wrote, "The North has not changed me. I am as sweet, unassuming as ever. I still crave food a la Mexico. I have a passion for Cokes. Can't stand bad movies. Double features, too. Think my li'l Ford is positively the nuts. Benny Goodman is still out of this world. Ditto that man Dorsey. Nothing finer than a tip-topper A-1 steak. A little on the rare side. Taxes to smash the Axis are fine. Set 'em on their axis." Conrad was making up for lost courtship time; Katherine was in step. The custom back then was to signal your devotion by applying the love letter's stamp upside down. In July, Katherine affixed her stamp that way for the first time. Conrad soon wrote back: "And I *did* notice the upper right-hand corner of [the] envelope. The ol' upside-down business of the stamp. Oh, yes!"

By early July, he mentioned engagement rings. Still, the long-distance courtship continued, with every letter revealing more of his personality. Katherine surely noticed that his letters were knowledgeable and virtually error-free, and that he wrote about literary subjects and his favorite writers – Elizabeth Barrett Browning, Oliver Wendell Holmes, William Shakespeare, and Charles Dickens, among others. His favorite popular author was Robert Service, whose poems of the Yukon and Alaska provided comic relief. To counterpoint that, he read the *New Yorker*, calling it "one of the best magazines published." His music tastes ran to Wagner as played by the New York Philharmonic.

Conrad was philosophical, too. Back in 1931, as his life values were still forming, he wrote his parents from summer camp: "We certainly had a nice swimming meet. I came in last but I at least made an effort." In August 1942, he saw a man fall from a 115-foot tower to his death. He wrote: "Proved to me how easy and foolish it is to act carelessly and how short this business of living is. To plan for the future is idle dreaming. To act today is concrete action – a definite example of my whole philosophy of life – forget yesterday, live today, don't worry about tomorrow." He wrote, "I have begun to adhere to a fundamental principle: happiness, fun, peace-of-mind is just where you find it." The party boy could find it everywhere, even in the use of money. To him, cash was "vitamin M."

He was clear on his views of social strata: "I think our move to Texas has been my guiding influence. The fact that people took us in without first examining our bank book, social calendar, and general previous 'case history' made a big impression on me. There were no discriminations. A girl was popular as she could be because of herself and not because of where she lived or how well off her family was. I went to Texas A&M. Even more of the same. No fraternities, no social lines of demarcation: just be yourself. I have formed friends in a class where there are no set standards. No clubs to brag about. No swanky automobiles to float around in. No 'big-shot connections.' " Instead, he would prefer his grandfather's "ideal spot up North in Michigan – a cabin nestled away in the pines right smack on a rushing river. Ideal!"

* * *

Of course, Conrad needed to learn more about Katherine than he had by observing her as a tomboy in high school. Though her letters from this period didn't survive, the picture is clear.

Katherine's personality developed from opposite poles. First, her father's absence during most of her life would leave her not only with regrets and emptiness but with what she later identified as a rejection complex. With that void, she could be excused for rejecting men. A go-it-alone attitude could have shaped her early years. Or she could have embraced men, especially strong leaders, to compensate for her loss. The second influence would have been her brothers. Though she did not have a father figure, she certainly had a formidable male contingent in the house. Tennille Jr., thirteen years older, could fill not only the brotherly role but also, in her high school years, almost the father role.

She lived with her mother, Maud Miller Henderson, and her grandmother, Katherine Fritter Miller. Her mother was almost forty at Katherine's birth. During Katherine's late teens she might have seemed more a grandmother than a mother. Whatever the ages, though, there was balance in the house.

Katherine learned to hold her ground both physically and mentally and to be competitive. Once, when her oldest brother went too far in harassment, she calmly chomped down on his leg just above the ankle, leaving perfect teeth marks for a week.

She was inclusive, seeking to bring all who were interested into her realm. This included coworkers, family, friends, and neighbors. All were welcome. She was artistic, showing remarkable talent for someone with no art education. Her drawings, designs, and artwork show innate talent.

She was a practical joker, at one point convincing everyone at a party that her late-arriving brother had lost almost all his hearing during the war, and so they should talk extra loudly to him. The look on Randall's face as friends shouted in his ear made the joke a success.

She was grounded by and in her family. An exasperating family, yes, but her family, and they came first.

She was drawn to Christ Episcopal Church, which would eventually give her life a true north. The war's result and her maturity would later in life put the church and her faith at the center of all she would achieve.

She was frugal, never wasting funds but occasionally allowing herself a well-planned if slightly frivolous treat.

She was energetic, resourceful, and full of plans. Maybe that's what inspired Conrad to write, after he saw a Bugs Bunny cartoon (*Stormy Weather* was the feature), "Thought of you when Bugs went through his stuff."

She was inquisitive, always looking for that new idea, new approach, or new style. One close friend reported that she was the first girl in San Antonio to wear blue jeans. Not surprising, then, that she would often quote Oliver Wendell Holmes: "Every now and then a man's mind is stretched by a new idea and never shrinks back to its former dimensions."

Despite this personality, if this relationship was to be successful she would have to nurture it on paper. Months would pass before she and Conrad would so much as hold hands.

Conrad left his job in September 1942 and moved to Dallas to join his parents and wait for his call into the service. He was ready. "I want to get out there myself. This job has to be done and the sooner the better," he wrote Katherine. That month he also planned their first date, October 23, a methodically scripted event in Dallas. Though Katherine had met his parents before, this would be their first official social event.

Imagine the pressure of any first date. Add the tension of Katherine taking the train to Dallas, mix in a set of parents, unfamiliar hotel rooms, and a romance that, at least on paper, had progressed to talk of marriage and children. And they were seeing each other for the first time in over two years. Every moment was made for disaster. Katherine boarded the train and went toward that future resolute in what it held for her.

Katherine's train was late, but shortly everything was "swell." In a letter months later, Conrad recalled: "Remember the first time I kissed you? Friday, October 23 – oh, how I wanted to and yet there was that unwritten law about first dates. Saturday, October 24, 1942. That was THE night. And you 'nuzzled.' Then, somehow, your face came up, and you looked at me, and I kissed you. It was that easy – so doggone nice. And you said – later – as well as I can remember, 'I don't know when I've been so completely kissed.' I loved you then, I love you a thousand times more now, darling, and always will."

Conrad quickly arranged a second date for November 7. He planned everything, being careful that he and Katherine would continue to observe all proprieties. His parents would again be chaperones. At the Adolphus Hotel in Dallas, he proposed. "Remember what happened to a 19-year-old San Antonio girl November 7, 1942? She was wearing a black dress and sitting by the dance floor."

Their engagement would continue long distance. "I can mail this letter before the 11 P.M. train leaves for San Antonio" was one option. Another was, "I tried to [telephone] you earlier but you weren't home. So then when I called again the operator said there would be a 2–3 hour wait."

Both sets of parents had to be dismayed at this courtship. Much later Katherine wrote:

Conrad and Katherine in downtown San Antonio on a winter day.

> *[Mama] caused me great anguish when [Conrad] and I were engaged. She had difficulty accepting the fact that I was grown and wanted to be married. She admired and loved Conrad III. But the shock of her daughter becoming a married woman and leaving home was severe. She insinuated delays into our marriage plans. I'm sure Conrad never knew. Mama probably never realized them herself. She was under great stress with three sons at war, and her anxiety, in the absence of a full-time husband to help her free me, is understandable.*
>
> *Actually, I don't believe Mama had any [ultimate] delaying effect on our marriage. [Conrad] was compelling, too, an even stronger influence, of course, than Mama. Repeat, Mama loved [Conrad]. She also feared being left alone.*

Whatever the reservations, the engagement was in no immediate danger of becoming a marriage. Conrad was headed for training, and Katherine went back to her civil service job at Fort Sam Houston. Whatever marriage plans they imagined would be on hold.

CHAPTER FOUR

─────────── ★ ───────────

Flying Through a Rainbow

America's military machine, sputtering to life in 1942, had need of materiel and men. The former was easy to manufacture per specifications. The latter were not so susceptible to a standardized military format. America's spirit includes independence, freedom, self-reliance, and individuality. The military needed men who would suppress these traits and replace them with dependence on others, subjection to authority, and acceptance of conformity. Achieving that transformation would not be easy.

For the Army Air Corps, fighter pilot training was even more complex. Trainees had to abandon their ingrained ideals, accept the military's version of a homogeneous and dependent fighting man, and then revert to self-involved, creative, and fiercely independent individualists and extroverts, all within eight months. That the program designed to achieve this was under a year old added to the problem. Nevertheless, graduates had to think on the fly and do so reflexively; the luxury of time was not a perk of the profession. This independent, split-second thinking would eventually permeate the military, including line soldiers, and today the military has little use for autocratic officers who don't or won't accept creative thinking from the troops.

The paradox between interdependent trainees and independent flyers was a burden to the military and a contradiction to the men. On one hand, they saw the military transform them into sycophants, shorn of excess hair and dressed identically. They would drill, seemingly without purpose, conform their living space to the military ideal, and receive demerits or gigs for failure to comply. But the military also taught them to fly using their instincts, allowed them to individualize their planes, and rewarded them for initiative.

Showing no signs that this paradox bothered him, Conrad arrived at the San Antonio Classification Center on January 10, 1943, and was appointed that day as an aviation cadet on special orders from

33

the recruiting district. The average recruit was twenty-six years old, weighed 144 pounds, and was 5' 8". Conrad was twenty-four years old, 140 pounds, and 5" 9".

"We listed our preferences. Pilot, navigator, bombardier in that order for me," he wrote Katherine. "As frankly as I can admit something I hate to admit, [training] not only looks like a tough row to hoe, but it's got me flat uncertain. [But] I'm so anxious to fly." To his father he wrote, "I thought when I was ten-years-old (Lindberg was quite a hero, remember?) it would be just about the biggest thing in the world for me if someday I could learn how to fly."

Not so fast. First he had to pass another eye exam. "[I'm] fearing [the eye exam] just a little." Later, he reported to Katherine: "I try reading the letters. This [right eye] is the eye that's all fouled up somewhere. I bear down. I manage to decipher some letters, somehow. Still haphazardly fumbling around trying to pick 'em. Somehow, I get the combination. Casually, [the examiner] turns to a major standing directly behind me and says, 'Well, this man checks 20/20 in both.' So I'll now, in all probability, be classified as a pilot." The problem was astigmatism in his right eye. But no one thought that it might one day affect his flying in critical circumstances.

Conrad was the wrong guy to force into military molds. His gigs piled up, an indicator of his disdain for seemingly unproductive procedures. "Have to walk off two tours (nine gigs), so I'm not falling into line too rapidly, thank the Lord," he wrote to his brother a month after training began. And within another week his classmates would call him "Mr. 'Gig' Netting." Not an auspicious beginning.

His order and neatness probably saved him from washing out. "We G.I.'ed the place this morning and it fairly sparkles. That's *one* thing I enjoy – cleaning up the place and keeping it looking clean. Really do fall in line in this department." Conrad could anticipate that flying also would be orderly, formulaic, and mathematical. Those qualities, added to his independent streak, would offset the excesses of militarism.

Why did Conrad want to be a pilot, other than to follow Lindbergh? Such a classification would almost guarantee combat, though the military needed many stateside trainers. He wrote his uncle: "[I want] a combat assignment and the sooner the better. Why? Lord – I wish

I knew. I've gone over the obvious reasons so many times I'm getting sick of it. Patriotism, revenge a friend, hell-for-leather stuff, don't give a damn, headlines. No, it isn't that – not all that rolled into one, either. And it isn't easy to admit that ninety percent of it isn't patriotism. It should be, I suppose. By golly, I simply cannot answer it. And strangely enough, being deeply in love with Katherine doesn't even remotely influence me one whit to stay over here."

Did many other trainees feel this way as well? If so, then the notion of the men signing on as patriots needs reexamining. Perhaps, as with all generations of combat pilots, they needed accomplishment, victory, independence, adventure, and a macho record to bring home. If they happened to be achieving their nation's goals, so much the better.

Oliver Wendell Holmes examined this phenomenon and extended his discussion to those who do not serve during war.

> We all know what the war fever is in our young men – what a devouring passion it becomes in those whom it assails. Patriotism is the fire of it, no doubt, but this is fed with fuel of all sorts. The love of adventure, the contagion of example, the fear of losing, the chance of participating in the great events of the time, the desire of personal distinction, all help to produce those singular transformations which we often witness, turning the most peaceful of our youth into the most ardent of our soldiers.
>
> But something of the same fever in a different form reaches a good many non-combatants, who have no thought of losing a drop of precious blood belonging to themselves or their families. Some of the symptoms we shall mention are almost universal; they are as plain in the people we meet everywhere as the marks of an influenza, when that is prevailing.
>
> The first is a nervous restlessness of a very peculiar character. Men cannot think, or write, or attend to their ordinary business. They stroll up and down the streets, or saunter out upon the public places. We confessed to an illustrious author that we laid down the volume of his work which we were

reading when the war broke out. It was as interesting as a romance, but the romance of the past grew pale before the red light of the terrible present. Meeting the same author not long afterwards, he confessed that he had laid down his pen at the same time that we had closed his book. He could not write about the sixteenth century any more than we could read about it, while the nineteenth was in the very agony and bloody sweat of its great sacrifice.

Maybe the trainees' attitude changed once they saw the devastation of battle, the lifeless blocks of London leveled by the Luftwaffe. Maybe before a battle the desire to fight was centered on being macho, and in battle it turned to true patriotism.

They couldn't know it then, but they needed a polestar to keep them going, and patriotism was the most obvious one. As it developed, 17 percent of battle deaths during World War II were airmen, a wildly disproportionate number given their numbers in the military. Of those Army Air Corps (later the Army Air Forces) battle deaths, 69 percent were accidental. The book *Deadly Sky* reported, "Asked if they would choose to sign up for combat flying if they had it to do all over again, ninety-three percent of fighter pilots answered yes."

Conrad arrived in Uvalde, Texas, ninety miles from San Antonio, for Primary (Pilot) Training, Class 43-I, in March 1943. He wrote: "This place is a country club. It's more than that. I spend lots of time around the pool, volleyball courts, and just generally sunning around the place. I'm in excellent condition. What a change from January 1, 1943." Despite his apparent incompatibility with the military, he was satisfied with his progress.

Soon he was in the air, although at first an instructor flew the plane. To Katherine he wrote: "Real thrill up there today. Got in forty-three minutes dual. A good start. They're paying me [to fly]!" And "We are on a rugged Aircraft Recognition course – 1/100 of a second on a screen to identify the plane." To his brother: "After 10:10 hours, he gave it to me alone – SOLO – and brother if you don't think it's an experience to stop all others, you're crazy."

As he tracked every minute of flying time in the flight log that would follow him throughout his military career, he found he had favorite types of flying. To Katherine: "I like to fly close to the ground – 500'. That's what the fellows can't understand – why it is that I get such a bang out of low work and detest high altitude stuff. Beats me." This low-level training would prove crucial in his combat flying.

At times he had a reality check. His mentor wrote him, "Con, flying military aircraft is dammed dangerous business." Within a month Conrad wrote to his father, "That phrase 'stay-on-the-ball' – Dad, that's the idea of this game. Because just slip once, and brother, that is all." And if that slip came from marginal eyesight? Well, the military was not short of eye exams. "We have another '64' eye examination tomorrow morning and I wouldn't give two bits for my chances of passing it." But he did.

Still walking on air because his avocation had become his vocation, he graduated to basic training in San Angelo, Texas, about 215 miles from San Antonio. By now his training spanned all types of conditions, including night flying. To Katherine: "What a thrill! You absolutely cannot see a doggone thing [flying at night]. It's pitch dark – oh, you see the blue flame coming from the exhaust and your instruments, etc., but you'd be surprised how inky black it is. But, darling, looking straight up – oh, it is beautiful! Stars by the million – and shooting stars, too."

After nine weeks at San Angelo, Conrad graduated and was promoted to advanced training in Mission, Texas, where his father had come during the Depression ten years before. In advanced training, students would get their final test in the P-40, a tactical plane, not a trainer, before being assigned to their first units.

Flying was electrifying for Conrad, and energizing, too. "I was up among several huge rain clouds, and there, off to my right, was a rainbow. You know how a rainbow looks from the ground – a semicircle? Well, up there it's a big circle – complete, and with the brightest rainbow circumscribed by larger and fainter rainbows. I flew around and around it for a while, and then flew right smack into it. It's just another one of those indescribable thrills of flying."

CHAPTER FIVE

———————— ★ ————————

"Three or Four Boys
and a Goat Ranch"

During World War II the common bond of Americans was separation: brothers from parents and siblings, fathers from wives and children, and, of course, young lovers from each other. Anne Ridler, in *The Lustre Jug,* writes: "[War] was not only a separation from normal life, from possessions, [but] a separation of husband from wife, friend from friend, [and] a separation of past from future. Usually, the past runs into the future so that you do not . . . know where one ends and the other begins: but war isolates the present . . . , presses the past into one concept, the time before the war began, and puts the future, the time when it will be ended, far off."

Each separation brought adversities, some more manageable than others. For brothers without wives or girlfriends, the adventure could be exciting and fulfilling. For fathers with budding careers and mortgaged homes, separation created burdens that might be as much financial as emotional. For young lovers like Katherine and Conrad, the separation was the end of the world.

Despite that, they were lucky that Conrad trained in San Antonio and South Texas, keeping him near Katherine. When their respective parents sought South Texas as their choice to raise families, they might have had a number of reasons. One prevailing reason was probably the weather, which though hot in the summer was pleasant the rest of the time, without the likelihood of hurricanes, as in Galveston, or of snow, as in Detroit. The semiarid climate meant only occasional inclement weather.

This was noticed by the Army Air Corps, which as early as 1916 created an air base in San Antonio and within a few years had four important bases ringing the city. When World War II required maximum training in minimum days, the Army Air Corps knew what part of the country could deliver – San Antonio.

When Conrad entered training, he and Katherine had been engaged for two months. They wrote to each other daily, as they would throughout the war. Some have called these war years the last glorious age of the love letter. Even when Conrad was at the San Antonio Classification Center for just a few weeks, he wrote every day. Phone calls were an unaffordable luxury. On one occasion his letter was postmarked on base at 3 p.m. while the delivering post office postmarked it at 4:30 p.m. the same day. Presumably, the letter would then be delivered to her home. All for ten cents.

But the method of communication wasn't that important. Being in communication was. And their letters were filled with talk of the future, of being with each other, of marriage and children. Conrad wrote:

> *Just imagine! Actually living with the girl I miss so terribly now. Actually getting our lives so interwoven with each other that nothing on this earth can separate us. Darling, there is something for us after this business is all over – our love for each other. Surely we should be looking forward to the most marvelous future two people could hope for. Just you and me. With a house. And three or four boys. Something to come back to – ever stop and think about that? .*
>
> *I hope that when this business is over and I do come back there will be more than just a case of coming back. I mean it this way, darling: I want to come back with a definite idea of stability, happiness, and above all, the love of our children so closely akin to that of our love for each other that we will be a family – in every sense of the word. Together – working together, playing together, laughing and crying together. But always as one, each sharing the laughs and joys, the tears and disappointments of the other. Looking forward to the most marvelous future two people could hope for. Darling, why a war? Why not just you and me together always, never without each other? Why? Gosh, I love you.*
>
> *When I get to feeling that I've had all I can stomach – all the pressure I can bear – I think of you. It's a fact, I think of us – together. Of all the plans we're making. Of the kids. Of so much more than Preflight. The Army Air*

Corps. The war. And then I get to feeling better. Because,
darling, whether you realize it or not, you and you alone
are pulling me through this thing. Don't ever forget it. And
because I love you so terribly much, I'd do anything in this
world for you.

And when that day comes [when this training is over],
then it's you and me, for life.

Katherine and Conrad saw each other in San Antonio and Uvalde by making elaborate plans to skirt the regulations, save gasoline coupons, carpool with other sweethearts, and make sleeping arrangements with officers' wives when the visit included an overnight stay. Conrad would send Katherine an occasional gift, including, for her twentieth birthday, Russian Leather perfume.

The daily letters continued. Wrote Katherine, an accomplished writer at twenty: "I am anxious but not, no never, impatient for this war to end, because I know that through the years, you and I will have what so many people can never find – a happy, gloriously happy marriage, and nice children. Perhaps they won't be the future presidents of anything, but they will have as a background a priceless quantity of love. What does it matter if we are never, well, even 'comfortably fixed,' if our children can have the security of the knowledge that they are our very much wanted, very much loved treasures?"

Having broached the subject of children before they were engaged, now was no time to stop. Conrad wrote: "Our dreams? They will come true, Katherine. They've just got to, that's all. I mean, we want those boys of ours – four – to grow up with us as their parents, don't we? Darn right." Early on they discussed a name, her preference being Conrad John Netting IV. He wrote: "Just think, Conrad IV – what a name tag the kid will be blessed with. 'Tough break, Conrad IV, but I tried my best to tell your mother not to hang it on you.' "

And a few weeks later: "I'm 100 percent in favor of this business of a fund for CJN IV. Have an idea he'll have it all spent before he's a year old. Sure do like to daydream about our son. He is going to be one fine boy if he turns out as we plan, won't he? I'm eager as the devil to be able to be so awfully proud when I say, 'That's my son!' "

Sometimes reality broke through. Conrad wrote: "Why do you think we've planned on children – right from the beginning? [I want a child] right away – as soon as possible. I want it this way for a very good reason, Katherine: I want you to have our child while I'm away. And I guess you know why."

Conrad also had big plans for a goat ranch near Sabinal, Texas, about seventy miles from San Antonio. This idea probably came from Katherine's friends, Margaret and David Habermacher, who owned such a place. To Katherine: "No question about it, I'm sold on this [flying] business. Oh, we'll have our el rancho grande all right, but there must be a plane along with it. After all, I've got to teach you and the children to fly, don't I?" To his parents: "If this [war] business was over tomorrow morning, I'd be down near Sabinal tomorrow afternoon dickering for [a ranch]. Both Katherine and I are dead set on a ranch with goats, sheep, and a family." Meanwhile, he bought some sheep from David, who some months later sent him $2.45 in proceeds from their mohair.

Before any of this could happen, they had to be married. In March 1943, early in his training schedule, Conrad was considering their options. "Either we get married while I'm a cadet, or it's no go. It's just that I cannot see it any other way. You certainly do not deserve to wait as long as it would take me to get that commission . . . You're my anchor." He followed that by writing: "Do you feel as though we wouldn't get off to a good start by getting married right after I get my wings [about October 28]? Do you feel as though we should wait until after the war?"

Feeling the pressure of time and war, the date moved forward. Katherine wrote on May 1, "How'd you like to get married just before you finish Basic [in late July]?" He wrote back, "As you decide, I abide," and suggested July 26. Then he recanted and suggested July 20 or 21. To his parents: "Reason? We know now that immediately on graduation we will be assigned to duty. No leaves, no grand honeymoons, nothing. So we have decided to get married while we will still be able to have some time together, however short." In his next letter, May 30, he found a date agreeable to both of them. "How about the twenty-fourth – it's a Saturday, you know and for all I know we wouldn't have any Sunday flying. Or say a week earlier – the seventeenth? Hey – the seventeenth! What do you say? I think that would be the best! And now we're going to be married so that another generation might have a chance to live."

Once the date was fixed, Conrad got busy. His Episcopalian roots surfaced and, while in San Angelo, he found Emanuel Episcopal Church. He wrote on June 5, six weeks before the proposed date: "I spoke to the rector, Mr. [Phillip] Kemp, and all's arranged for a 7:30 wedding [on July 17], very simple, in the church itself. He was once assistant rector at St. Mark's [in San Antonio]." That left Katherine and her family to make the bridal arrangements. He wrote, "The idea of your coming out at noon on the seventeenth is O.K. I guess if that's the way you want it." Somehow, on extremely short notice, Katherine's family mobilized. Her father returned from Mexico to give her away, her brother Jimmie gave the reception, Randall was best man, and her oldest brother Tennille, and his wife, Frances, gave a shower in San Antonio.

Conrad got rooms for everyone at the St. Angelus Hotel and reserved a room for himself and his bride at the Cactus Hotel, San Angelo's only high-rise building. No one from the Netting family could attend, as all were in Detroit, or on war duty.

The Henderson brothers had always welcomed Conrad as a fourth brother, so to know he would now be a brother-in-law was an easy adjustment. Katherine's mother, Maud, though welcoming, must have wondered about the long-distance courtship, the engagement after one date, and the hurried wedding plans of her youngest child, only twenty. It must have been hard to accept that a war could cause these short circuits in social customs. (She married in 1909, well before World War I.) On the surface, at least, parents on both sides seemed to respect and admire their new in-laws.

Few friends attended the wedding, a disappointment but not unexpected. One close friend did send a telegram: "Can't make it tonight. Don't wait up for me." Little is known of the wedding, as no pictures survive or may ever have existed. No record exists, either, of the bride's dress or the reception. The honeymoon lasted twelve hours, with Conrad back on base the following afternoon and the Henderson family with the new Mrs. Conrad J. Netting III back in San Antonio.

As the letters resumed, the glow from their new partnership was evident. Conrad wrote in August, "After the wedding, [I remember] just looking at you and saying over and over again to myself, 'This is my wife, my very own forever!' "

* * *

Katherine and Conrad had made many life-altering decisions in a short time, each creating a tension that was palpable. First Conrad decided to leave Texas A&M. Then he left Mobilgas. Next he volunteered and applied for combat. For her part, Katherine had agreed to marry him and reluctantly supported his wartime decisions. Couples in any era make many of these decisions. Unique to wartime, however, and to this war especially, was the compressed time frame. Time was a luxury Conrad and Katherine did not have.

They had another decision to make: when to have a baby. Instinct and a deep respect for family lineage told them, no doubt, to begin a new generation. Still, Conrad's risks as a combat fighter pilot must have caused them to think twice. With a baby at home, Katherine would have added responsibilities, especially financial. And, thinking the unthinkable, if Conrad did not return, how could she cope, especially with no college degree, no career prospects, and no adequate income?

The decision was not entirely theirs to make. Medicine then offered no control over conception. Timing was everything. Their decision was to try for a baby at once, and apparently they were in concert on this from the beginning. The war, of course, weighed heavily. What had been bravado during courtship was now marital reality. Conrad wrote: "I'm much too busy living this day, hoping to heaven I'll be here for tomorrow but not going head over heels planning for it. [Our friends] say for us to get our happiness while we can." The pall of mortality was evident in their letters.

The propriety of the time did not allow for the realities of propagation. The Victorian generation was still influencing society. The Roaring 20s were a distant memory, made more so by the cold realities of the Depression. In Hollywood, the Hayes Code, setting standards for what movies could show and tell, was less than ten years old. Even couples, in their letters, skirted the realities and employed the code words of the day: the curse, p.g., and M dresses. Conrad wrote in August: "I'm terribly disappointed [a baby] 'isn't.' I had my hopes up pretty blamed high, believe me. But then, I really should have known better – according to the time-schedule, it couldn't pos-

A portrait of Katherine and Conrad Netting taken shortly after his commissioning in October 1943.

sibly work out our way, could it?" Katherine responded: "Think I need some vitamins. I have *no* pep. Perhaps it is like that corny song, 'I need Vitamin U.' "

After their wedding, Conrad had to complete one more segment of training after he left San Angelo in late July. Advanced pilot training for him was in Mission, Texas, at Moore Field, and lasted until October 1, after which he was commissioned and received his wings, another nine-month wonder. Katherine joined him for the ceremonies. He wore his new officer's uniform: "Got (1) blouse, (2) green [olive drab] shirts, (3) three khaki shirts, and (4) khaki trousers. $76 not including alterations."

Before leaving Mission, Conrad got his wish. "Since I, too, want combat and in the worst possible way, I asked for and got a combat assignment. I would judge that about half the class got combat, the rest instructor, ATC, TCC – I was lucky, I guess." In a prescient moment, he made an on-point prediction in a letter to his uncle: "We're all fairly itching for this P-51B which is as fast and much more maneuverable than the famed P-38. Just wait until this new 51 sees combat!"

After commissioning, they returned to San Antonio on leave. "The train leaves out [of McAllen] at 6:20 P.M. getting in San Antonio [245 miles away] the next morning." To his uncle Conrad wrote: "Katherine and I spent four days at home in San Antonio visiting friends, etc. Then we went on over to New Orleans for a sort of combination honeymoon, leave, vacation or what have you. It lasted just five days, but I can readily assure you I cannot remember five days that flew by quite as rapidly as did those. Nor can I remember five days that were any happier, any more complete."

Katherine felt the same: "Darling, I want very much to have your child – and not just one – I want our lives to fill the specifications we have drawn up – but, if they shouldn't, if every dream were shattered, every hope crushed – I should never complain. I have been as happy with you in our few pitiful weeks of being *actually* together as any other woman in a whole lifetime. I never realized before to what awe-inspiring heights marriage can carry two people. It isn't the actual physical marriage so much as the most sustaining knowledge that the person you love returns that love with equal fervor that is so magnificent. My greatest desire is to make you happy – nothing else is important. You are paramount."

Lt. Conrad Netting III on leave in San Antonio.

More training followed, this time at Tallahassee, Florida, where the Army had the news Conrad wanted. He wrote to Katherine: "We are to be the first group to go through on an entirely new schedule and we're tagged (evidently and eventually) for a fighter-bomber outfit . . . . It does mean fighter-type aircraft." But his old nemesis followed him to Florida. "Some of us could barely read that eye chart, but we got 20/20 anyway."

Relieved to pass another eye exam, he signed on with the 57th Fighter Squadron of the 54th Fighter Group.

Conrad made impromptu plans for Katherine to join him. She arranged the trip: "Braniff [Airways] from San Antonio to Tallahassee is $63.70. I would leave on afternoon plane at 5:00 P.M. and arrive Tallahassee at 6:00 A.M. the next morning. The rate at the hotel [in Tallahassee] is $17.50 a week."

That trip never happened. After just five weeks in Tallahassee, Conrad transferred to Bartow, Florida, east of Tampa. He could have Katherine join him if she stayed off base. The base had no facilities for married couples, especially when the stay would be a matter of weeks. Getting there was an effort. Katherine wrote: "I called and made reservations on Braniff for the twenty-third [of November]. I leave at 3:40 P.M., arrive Dallas [300 miles away] about 7 P.M., and take off right away for Atlanta arriving about midnight. Then I get in Tampa at six in the morning." As it developed, her tickets were cancelled, probably because of the military's priority, and she spent three days on the train and bus.

In Bartow, Katherine and Conrad created a home, though it was a tourist court room with kitchenette. To them it was heaven on earth. His training allowed for a regular schedule and routine hours. Her days were filled writing letters home, tending to their clothes and shopping, and reading. At night, their dinners out together were answered prayers. And without benefit of television, Conrad would routinely fall asleep on the couch. Just before Christmas, Katherine wrote to both sets of parents and to siblings: "On the 4th of July 1944, another member of the Netting family is due to arrive. Conrad and I both are hoping for a boy, to be Conrad John Netting IV. But, I feel sure if 'it' is a girl, she won't be neglected."

Randall, the brother and best friend, responded that no one should be named that. Too big a mouthful. He suggested Conjon, a shortened version of the first two names. And for the parents to be, that nickname would stick.

The tourist court hearth couldn't last, of course, and in January Conrad received orders to head to New York and then overseas. The stress must have nearly immobilized Katherine, though it couldn't have come as a surprise. They made arrangements and decided she should take his car home. Not surprisingly, that trip, begun on Valentine's Day, was an adventure for Katherine, four months pregnant. She wrote Conrad:

> Ten miles [east] of Orange, Texas, we had a flat on the retread. Just as I was trying to change it on a wet gravel [shoulder], two men stopped and with their jack managed to get it off. I got to Orange, had the tire vulcanized and the man said the tire was gone. I looked inside and all the cording had come loose. He put a lot of stickum in and a relining and said that we might make San Antonio [320 miles away]. He said that the space was a good casing and it would be a darn good tire if I had it retreaded. Better than any 3rd grade I could buy. So, I am planning on having that one retreaded instead of getting a paper for it.
>
> Then we limped on at thirty-five miles an hour from Orange to within seventy miles of San Antonio. I noticed that the road seemed rough for a number of miles, and I even leaned out the window and saw that [the tire] was a ways up. I drove on it that way for about thirty miles. Then I pulled over to the side of the road, and looked at it. It was still up, but it looked funny. I started out on the highway, and BANG! So, I guided the car around to the gravel again. I managed to jack the car up pretty high but I had to dig the gravel out to get the spare on.
>
> Then I held my breath for two whole hours while I watched for [San Antonio]. Sure enough, it held up. I spent $6.00 on the relining and vulcanizing, and $14.84 on gas and oil [from Florida]. I drove over 1100 miles. So I think it was very cheap. And here I am like a collapsed balloon.

Katherine's emotions after this trip – she averaged forty miles an hour – were on overload. She was tackling marriage, parenting, and separation in just six months. Collapsed balloon was just the beginning. From San Antonio, she wrote Conrad: "Do you feel as 'halved' as I do? You know in the [Episcopal] Prayer Book where it says, 'Where two or three are gathered together in common supplication'? Well, Conjon and I make two, and we prayed all afternoon for you. Darling, I wouldn't care what happened to me or him or anyone if anything happened to you. So please – please – be careful."

Conrad, meanwhile, was suffering through his all-expense paid trip to New York "on a special train . . . in a dirty tourist Pullman." He arrived in Brooklyn at Fort Hamilton, a place, he wrote, that "is a typical G.I. fort in the old peace days that hasn't heard of Air Corp's regulations – any type of uniform goes."

Though he was poised to leave for England, his orders had not come through. He wrote to his parents: "I'm so eager to go it's unexplainable. And yet, I want to be with Katherine, naturally. But far above this feeling, is the urge to go across and get into this thing. Not because I like a scrap or because I personally have a grievance against the enemy. I frankly believe it's because I want to put to the test all the gosh-awful training I've gone through in the last thirteen months." Was he putting the war above his bride? He had a lifetime to spend with Katherine, but only until war's end in the military. He would finish off this adventure, then return to her for life. He wrote her: "Never once think I won't take care of this guy. He loves you far too much to miss out on the post-war business of raising a family."

CHAPTER SIX

———— ★ ————

Debden Airfield, England

The movement of men between stateside posts and overseas was just one of the behind-the-scenes World War II successes. Before computers, the military kept track of everything – pay, allotments, equipment, and bodies – largely by hand, and for millions of men. The logistical challenges were daunting. To its credit, the military got the job done. Conrad was never forgotten, misplaced, or off track. With unimaginable precision, he was processed through nine stateside assignments, from the San Antonio Classification Center in January 1943 until now, February 1944, at Fort Hamilton.

Years before, he had left behind the comfort of San Antonio's neighborhoods; his friends and family were scattered around the world. Replacing them were Army buddies. At least one man was to track Conrad's training course step for step. Joseph A. (Pat) Patteeuw (a Belgian/Flemish name pronounced PATTY-you) found himself alongside Conrad from San Antonio to Fort Hamilton. Pat would take care of Conrad and his family in ways neither could foresee.

If your parents had died when you were nine and you had since lived with your older sister and her husband and children, much like a boarder, you would not see Pearl Harbor as an interruption to your life, but rather as the opportunity for one. Pat Patteeuw was in line at the draft station on December 8, 1941, as Congress was preparing articles of war against Japan. When he reached the counter the sergeant asked if he had a job. Pat wondered what a job had to do with enlisting. "Yes," he answered, giving the inquisitor a flinty stare. That meant the Army wouldn't take him. They preferred those without jobs, a bid to use the war as a tonic against the Depression. Promised another opportunity, Pat returned later as planned and was in. Within days, he quit his job.

Cocky but not arrogant, Pat needed a place to be. Unlike Conrad, who had generations of family, Pat had no parents, no wife – no familial ties. Alone and highly flexible, he could blow with the wind, landing wherever it carried him.

He had much in common with Conrad. Both were from Detroit. "We were both eastsiders," he would say. Though Pat was four years younger, he and Conrad had similar scrawny physiques and dark hair, and both were of average height. Pat's oversized jaw and Midwest nasal accent were immediately noticeable. His build, background, and brassiness were just what the Army Air Corps needed, but not for an aircraft mechanic, Pat's initial classification. Soon enough he would be a pilot. Once Pat arrived at the San Antonio Classification Center, Conrad was never far away.

✶ ✶ ✶

Conrad's ten days in New York were filled with irony. He was released early every day because he had no assignment – except waiting. Almost nightly he saw the sights and lights, plays and movies. He ate like never before. He wrote to Katherine: "You should have seen [us] when we climbed up those subway stairs for the first time and saw [Times Square]. Mouths gaping wide, just standing there. Stood at 42nd Street and Broadway for fully fifteen minutes." On other nights, he went to see Raymond Massey in Lovers and Friends ("at half-price!"), which he called excellent, Arsenic and Old Lace, and Life With Father. It was impossible, he wrote, to see Oklahoma. One night he saw Stars on Ice at Rockefeller Center and reported it "wonderful."

He took his ease at the Hotel Astor on Times Square and, relaxing in the Columbia Room, probably listened to José Morand and his orchestra. Because of the influx of single men, the Astor Hotel felt compelled to announce on each of its tables: "We ask our male guests, both military and civilian, to refrain from 'mixing' with unescorted ladies at other tables. Compliance with this request will save embarrassment to you, to us and to the ladies involved."

When the Astor got dull, Conrad went to the "Ritz Carlton and had a few snifters," and from there to see Xavier Cougat and his thirty-two-piece orchestra. He sampled food of every variety, managing to find Mexican food one night, though not San Antonio–style.

Here was a chance to enjoy time with Katherine, as he had in Florida, and yet he couldn't. She was a collapsed balloon and he was on the town. His letters suggest the turmoil he felt about this, though hers encouraged him to see and do all he could. He stopped by the Elizabeth Arden store and bought Katherine a present, noting that "Fifth Avenue took my breath away."

Within a few weeks, Conrad, Pat, and the others shipped out. Pat said: "The boat we took overseas was in a huge convoy. It was a converted Argentine meat boat. Took eleven days. We sailed from New York." Conrad wrote to Katherine: "We did have good meals coming over. It was entirely British – service deluxe, et al – but it wasn't bad."

Pat said later that the men were sardines on that boat, even the officers. Their bunks were one-by-twelve boards hung from the ceiling in stacks, with room enough to lie flat and not turn over. The officers' wardroom was more commodious and supported a bridge game or two that would continue for days. Pat said, "I didn't play bridge at the time, so I was a kibitzer. Conrad was probably playing and I was kibitzing him. At some point I took a hand while another officer went to the head. I played bridge for the next ten days and have never played bridge again in my life. It's one of those things you do, and then you don't do it anymore."

By mid-March 1944, Conrad and Pat were in the 555th Fighter Squadron, 496th Fighter Group, in Goxhill, Lincolnshire, a replacement unit. Such units received men from the United States, processed their paperwork, and matched them with units that had openings (a discreet term for deaths). Though too busy, anxious, and excited to notice, they were replacing destroyed assets in forward units like so many tanks or planes.

Goxhill was a typical Nissen hut station. The men lived in huts named for Lt. Col. Peter N. Nissen, who developed the easily built shelters during World War I. They were dismal metal buildings shaped like the lengthwise half of a coffee can. The men slept around a pot-bellied stove. The W.C. was down the road. Conrad wrote: "We live eleven to a Nissen hut but with one stove. The thing is pretty drafty and chilly."

March would have been raw and bone-chillingly cold, especially for men who had spent the last year in near-100 degree Texas heat.

It snowed on April 1. Funny how in all that swaggering talk back in training – duty, service, and glory – no one mentioned having one belching stove and living in a metal hut. And where were the planes? They hadn't flown a plane in over a month and would need hours in the air to feel confident again. But this was a temporary assignment; maybe their luck would turn.

* * *

Just one of the many blessings God gave the Allies was East Anglia, the undulating expanse of England northeast of London, and the closest point to the European continent and thus Germany. About the size of Rhode Island, it had many dells and pastures that gave livelihood to generations of Anglican farmers. One was A. C. Kettley. Legend has it that in 1937 a Royal Air Force (RAF) plane was forced down on his land while he was fishing for brook trout at one of his ponds. When Mr. Kettley challenged the flyer as to his intentions, he said he was scouting for airfields and was testing out this particular meadow.

Lt. Conrad Netting, center, with Bartow, Florida pilot training buddies Tom McDill, left, and Pat Patteeuw.

And, he continued, he found the land suitable, if not perfect – the pond would have to go – and would make arrangements immediately with London. After a further exchange, which remains unrecorded, the land was secured. Mr. Kettley had the distinction of owning the land on which the first RAF prewar fighter base was built.

Just a kilometer or two from Debden, a mini-village southeast of Cambridge, that first airbase would soon have plenty of company. By the start of the war in September 1939, the RAF had built fifteen other aerodromes and five satellite operations in East Anglia. By war's end, the area would have 107 airfields designed for either fighters or bombers. All were situated so each field could get its units airborne without much danger of its airspace overlapping with that of other fields. Everyone hoped the engineers got that right.

The German Luftwaffe attempted to destroy these fields and in 1940 attacked Debden with a Dornier Do-17 bomber. They damaged nothing more than the runways, but that was enough. The runways were patched just enough to get them back into service. Pat Patteeuw recalled: "Every time we took off, just before you'd get airborne, you'd hit that bump [from the patch]. And as our plane would start up, then it'd come back down again. But the [patch] on the other runway was so bad we never could even use it."

Over the years, the RAF saw Debden as its model aerodrome and improved it with permanent brick buildings designed to hold 2,000 men in two fighter squadrons. The unofficial archive of the Debden airfield, *1000 Destroyed*, says: "Debden was a permanent RAF station, which meant steam-heated brick buildings, tennis and squash courts, billiard room, napkin rings, flowers, waitresses, civilian orderlies called batmen, and RAF silverware. So, Debden existed as an oasis of luxury and comfort. The food was superior to that offered by some deluxe London hotels."

When Germany's Luftwaffe was laying waste to London in 1940, many American men sought to help, but since the United States was not at war there were no American units to join. Undeterred, these latter-day cowboys enlisted in the RAF or Royal Canadian Air Force (RCAF). The RAF designated a squadron as the cowboys' unit. Named the Eagle Squadron, it quickly became famous. The 1942 movie about it stars Robert Stack. So heroically and selflessly did those Americans fight for another country that the Eagle Squadron became legendary.

The perfect place to house these men was, of course, Debden. The over-the-top creature comforts were the ideal match for the over-the-top contribution of these Americans. Then, in September 1942, after America was on a full wartime footing, the RAF and RCAF relinquished control of the Eagle Squadron to the Army Air Corps, which renamed it the 4th Fighter Group. The three independent Eagle squadrons (Nos. 71, 121, and 133) were renumbered the 334th, 335th, and 336th Army Air Corps squadrons.

To put Debden's size into perspective, consider this analysis from *1000 Destroyed*: "The population of the 4th Group at Debden consisted of some 1,500 officers and men. (A group is the counterpart of a regiment.) Relatively few are pilots. A group is ordinarily composed of three squadrons, which commonly fly sixteen planes each. Each of these squadrons has more than 200 enlisted men. To the three fighter squadrons is added a 'service group' of three squadrons, plus non-flying officers." Of course, those 1,500 slots (3 percent of which were pilots) would indicate full strength. Replacements were needed almost daily. Conrad and Pat, with nineteen other pilots, arrived on April 4 to help fill the need.

After the cold, impersonal Nissen huts, Conrad and Pat must have been astonished when, they saw what their adventure at Debden would be like. Not only had they trained together for over a year, now they would be roommates. Conrad wrote home:

> *The deal here [at Debden] far exceeds even my most remote ideas of what we would get. The [American prepared] food is positively A-1, and what I mean, after the food we had where we were, plus K-rations on the trains, it means a lot to us. The mess is excellent and we get real honest-to-goodness eggs pretty regularly. If Uvalde was a country club, this certainly beats even my wildest hopes. The place is positively luxurious with the accent on comfort. Pat and I have moved over here in the club! How we ever squeezed in ahead of so many guys I'll never*

know, but we're here. Right in the very center of everything and the best possible deal imaginable.

This was once the old Eagle Squadron and it had a whale of a lot of tradition then, and still has. We live in [buildings] that look and are very much like fraternity houses at a northern university because they're brick and very big. And some rooms are for two, some four, some single. Each is entirely different. The Officers' Club reminds me very much of a Country Club up north [in Michigan] – just like Red Run. Just exactly. Extremely comfortable and genteel.

Pat was no less impressed. "The place where we ate had tables with waitresses. It had to be the best quarters in Europe by far."

Both airmen went to work to personalize their room. Conrad's letters to Katherine boasted: "This afternoon Pat and I worked on our map – spreading it clear across a wall. It has to be pieced together from sectional maps, but when we get all through, we'll be able to keep track of where we've been. You ought to see the way we have one complete side of our room covered with England, Europe, and the Scandinavian Countries. Scale is 1" = 16 mi. so you can see how big it is. Represents plenty of work piecing 'em all together, and part of it extends over the ceiling yet!"

Imagine if you were to learn there was one more comfort that you had only seen in the movies. Pat explained:

> The way you got a shoeshine is when you went to bed at night, you took your shoes off, and you put them outside the door in the corridor. And you closed the door. And then in the morning, when you woke up, your shoes were there all shined. The batman did it. If you wanted your clothing washed, you dropped it on the floor. If you wanted it dry-cleaned, you threw it over the bed when you left. So when you'd come back, it was all washed, dry-cleaned, and hung back up in the closet.
>
> A batman is a servant for British army officers. Nothing like we have in the military in the United States. But the British do. And usually, they're

higher ranking officers, and they have to pay them themselves. He's a personal valet. And he took care of us. He made our bed. He would get awful mad if we tried to do it. We'd make the bed and he'd straighten it out, and he took great joy in that. We were warned not to tip him more than one pound a month, equivalent then to four dollars.

Conrad wrote that it was "luxury. With a capital L."

———— ★ ————

CHAPTER SEVEN

Conjon IV –
A Magnificent P-51

The 4th Fighter Group was part of the Eighth Air Force, the largest assembly of aircraft in history. According to *1000 Destroyed*: "By early 1944 the Eighth Air Force had embarked on an offensive to destroy the German fighter strength in the air and on the vine. The fighters . . . were picking fights with the Luftwaffe while the bombers . . . were destroying aircraft factories to prevent replacements. German fighter strength had reached alarming, peak proportions and it had to be knocked out before an invasion of the Continent could be undertaken." At full strength, the Eighth Air Force could send on a day's operation 5,000 aircraft, a virtual blanket over East Anglia. In them could be 20,000 or more young men. Two of them were likely Conrad and Pat.

Before they signed in at Debden, the 4th Fighter Group was on its way to making history. Its mission was to escort bombers that attacked factories, submarine pens, V-weapon sites, and other targets in France, the Low Countries, and Germany. Ancillary missions were to attack the enemy's air power by strafing and dive-bombing airfields and to hit troops, supply depots, roads, bridges, rail lines, and trains. The 4th was the first to attack the enemy in the skies over Berlin and Paris, and was the first, in July 1943, to fly into German territory.

The group did this with breathtaking success. Consider the accolades in *Aces Against Germany*: "The 4th Fighter Group alone was upholding the honor of American fighter units in England [from September 1942 to April 1943]. The 4th Fighter Group was as aggressive and aggressively led a fighter unit as ever fought in a war." More praise came from *Little Friends*: "The 4th at Debden became the highest-scoring fighter group in the USAAF. A German propaganda statement called them the 'Debden Gangsters.' " The 336th Fighter Squadron, the squadron Conrad and Pat would join, held the record for the highest score of any squadron for a single mission (April 5, 1944): twenty-six enemy aircraft destroyed, two probably destroyed, and sixteen damaged.

As the reputation of these gangsters grew, so did their mystique. Over time they developed a slang that distinguished them from other units, including calling their planes "kites," a term that vastly understated the complexity of the aircraft. To "prang" their kite meant they had cracked it up, a far gentler term than "wrecked." A "show" was a mission, and a "white diamond" was a fresh egg and just as rare. Most poignant, perhaps, was "N.Y.R.," for "not yet returned," the classification assigned to a pilot who was not back on schedule but not yet listed as missing in action.

To win against Germany, the pilots had to have the right equipment and, in another God-given advantage, they got it. Before February 1944, the Army Air Corps pursued the Luftwaffe using P-47 Thunderbolts, which landed in the history books when they flew over the German border in July 1943. The P-47 was a workhorse earning its credentials daily. In February 1944, however, P-51 Mustangs, Model B, arrived to replace the Thunderbolts. Within days, the P-51s (the "P" stood for pursuit) were over Berlin for the first time. Reichmarshal Hermann Goering said on March 4, 1944, when he saw the scarlet-nosed Debden Mustangs over Berlin, "We have lost the war."

What was so astonishing about this machine? Not much, other than the fact that it helped save the Eighth Air Force from extinction. Noted one report, "it was probably the best piston-engine fighter of the war." Another stated, "it was the last and greatest propeller-driven fighter which, when the British fitted it with their own superb engine, the legendary Merlin, could outperform any other." It just flat looked the part: sleek, shiny, silvery, and aerodynamically fit, it had no detractors. In January 1944 Time magazine reported the pilots' view of the Mustang: "Air men wagged their heads and wondered whether, at long last, this was it – the single-seater that had everything. . . . It was fast, agile and an 'honest' aircraft (i.e., with no eccentric handling traits)."

The P-51 came from mixed lineage. The British in 1941 desperately needed a new fighter, but their factories weren't safe from Luftwaffe attack. The British found that all American factories were busy building planes for America – except one. North American Aviation had capacity and a design. In record time – 120 days – it produced the first plane to use an Allison engine. When that engine failed to meet standards, the British matched their Merlin engine with the P-51 Mustang body and success was born.

Over time, and with a thoroughly trained pilot, the P-51 would eliminate the Luftwaffe. Its mission would eventually shift from air-to-air combat to air-to-ground. Despite the glowing report in Time that "the Mustang proved itself a magnificent low-level strafer and locomotive-buster," it was not built for that purpose. The engine's liquid-cooling system was exposed to small arms fire during strafing attacks, making such pursuits deadly. The military, in late 1944, forbid strafing by the P-51s.

Though Conrad and Pat had trained on these planes in Florida, seeing them in action was altogether different. Conrad wrote home:

> I got a brand, spanking new [kite] with just ferry time on it, plus what is admittedly the best crew chief and assistant in the 336th Fighter Squadron. So, you can see how tickled I am about the whole deal. Only it's never been painted, and while I hate to see its slick, clean lines all covered with paint, it's for my own neck that I see the distinct advisability of painting it. We had some unpainted ones with us on yesterday's show, and they stood out like a sore thumb. I flew it for the first time it's been flown in England (crated up and boated over) today – and wrung it out but good, and it's just like a new car – sensitive, lovely, eager, marvelous. Oh, gosh – I'm sure happy about this.

Having a personal kite was an honor pilots had to earn, the ultimate status symbol and one they would go to almost any length to nurture. The assigned designation for Conrad's kite was VF-S. Those initials were painted in bold block letters behind the cockpit.

As was every pilot's dream, Conrad got to name his kite. Defying any notion that their unborn child might be a girl, he wrote, "I decided long ago that when I do get my own kite, it will be named 'Conjon IV.'" Naming your own kite was more exciting than handing out cigars. "The Conjon is Randall's abbreviation for Conrad John, and it follows that it had just better be a boy. Sure do want one. Damned good kite."

Katherine, amazed at his audacity, wrote back: "What if it is Virginia? Perhaps you had better call it something neutral like, well, like . . . Okay, so I can't think of anything. But hadn't you better call it just 'It' until July? Just for safety's sake?"

Ignoring that suggestion, Conrad responded: "Having a hell of a time getting the painter to put 'Conjon IV' on my kite. He'll put it under the exhaust stacks, but he's pretty busy putting Swastikas [one for each destroyed German plane] on others." Understandable since the 4th Fighter Group was busy setting records for destroyed German planes. Soon enough, the sign painter, Don Allen, found time to paint the name, presumably charging his usual fee of $35. What a switch, he probably thought, from the pin-up girls these fighter cowboys usually pick. It was certainly easier to paint. Just eight block letters.

The next day, as the men began to call him Conjon, just to tease him, Conrad must have wondered if he had acted too soon. What if, two months from now, the baby was a girl! He had insisted on Virginia if it was. But wasn't it proper for the world to have a Conrad IV in this long line of Conrad John Nettings that began in 1868? Still, what if they started calling him Virginia?

Three ingredients meshed at Debden to elevate it above other air bases: the posh accommodations, the P-51's flawless fit into its role, and the men of the 4th Fighter Group who, building on the Eagle Squadron legacy, were the best in their league. Conrad wrote to Katherine: "The thing that has completely sold us on the 4th Fighter Group is the attitude of the men. They're wonderful, every one of them. It's all on a cooperative basis with the new pilots given every possible bit of advantage plus a big helping hand. The Group is as relaxed and easy going as the law allows (uniform regulations just don't exist except in the evenings), but behind all this is an eagerness about flying that is plenty obvious."

New Debden pilots are shown in April 1944 at a pep talk in this photo from the *Illustrated London News* in May. Conrad Netting III is in front of the window at left, Pat Patteuuw in front of the window at right.

And to his parents: "The comradeship and general feeling of a cooperative spirit here is most welcomed – putting it mildly. Being able to talk with the Colonel as though he, also, were just a second lieutenant, for instance, is something new under the sun for us. And saluting! Well, we respect rank here, but nobody bends over backwards saluting, and that's something else that's most welcomed. Every man here is eager to help us, from our C.O. right on down to private, and you'd be surprised how much they all can help. It's wonderful."

Conrad and Pat would need the help. Decades later Paddy Barthropp, an RAF fighter pilot, recalled: "During World War II [the P-51 pilot] had total control of a 400 m.p.h. fighter and eight machine guns – with no radar, no auto-pilot, and no electronics. His aircraft carried ninety gallons of fuel between his chest and the engine. He often flew over 35,000 feet with no cockpit heating or pressurization. He endured up to six times the force of gravity with no G-suit. He had about three seconds in which to identify his foe, and slightly longer to abandon the aircraft if hit. He had no ejector seat. However, every hour of every day was an unforgettable and marvelous experience shared with some of the finest characters who ever lived."

Despite the assumption that pilots were rigidly independent, they did have to coordinate closely with other pilots. They went up on shows nearly every day, weather permitting. And the assignments were hardly milk runs. The shells from anti-aircraft artillery were called flak, named from the German for anti-aircraft gun *fl(ieger)a(bw her)k(anone)*, and it was a constant danger, especially for the bombers. Conrad wrote, "We picked up the bombers and escorted them home. One thing about these boys in the Forts [B-17 Fortresses] and Libs [B-24 Liberators] – never again will I derisively kid them in any way about their jobs – 'truck drivers,' etc. Not after what I saw yesterday. Those boys have one helluva time with flak and enemy fighters, and when you ride up above 'em and watch 'em take it (flak), then your kidding days are over. We keep fighters off them – as much as we can – but neither we nor anyone else can do anything about flak. They seem to just sit there and take it." They took it as long as they could, but 73 percent of Army airmen did not complete their duty tour of twenty-five missions.

About a month later, Conrad wrote Katherine: "Yesterday and today we helped make a little history, I guess. Two consecutive days over Berlin. The flak was terrifically concentrated. We avoided it as much as possible, but the 'big friends' worked right on through it. Sure gives a fellow a lot of respect for those boys." And on another occasion: "Yesterday I was in an all-time fighter group record, getting nine operations hours in one day, flying two shows. Was over Berlin, Paris, and London within those nine hours. Interesting – ?"

History was made when the P-51s first reached Berlin. Many say it was the beginning of the end. Yet Conrad and the others didn't know that. As Andrew Greig noted in *The Clouds Above*: "None of these people knew the outcome of anything – the War, the next week, who will survive and who won't . . . They are the most up-to-date people on the planet and still they don't know."

Later, to his parents, Conrad wrote, "You can't believe how unbelievably small that cockpit can get after four or five hours. That cockpit gets awfully tiny and I've found there is more than one position to sit in it. It's tiresome and monotonous only when nothing is doing, or 'stooging around' as we call it. But on a bounce or dodging flak – well, you don't have time to think about being tired. It's a great life and full of excitement."

He might call it excitement when writing to his parents, but to others it would register as terror. Consider his combat report (prepared in seven carbon copies) of April 24, 1944, detailing his activity over Frankfurt:

> Flack was all over and under us . . . The [Focke-Wulf] 190 . . . turned directly into me. The 190 was coming straight at me. . . . I fired a good burst at him and he passed directly under me, barely missing collision. I immediately turned left and looked behind me and saw this FW-190 spinning and obviously out of control, going straight in. I claim this FW-190 probably destroyed.

Another combat report would capture better than any fiction ever could a few minutes in the life of a combat fighter pilot. From May 29, 1944:

> I was flying Col. Blakeslee's No. 2 and we were weaving across the top of the lead box of bombers as they were heading out. I called in two bogies coming in from the bombers' 7 o'clock and to our 9 o'clock, about 2–3,000 feet below us. We immediately turned starboard. Col. Blakeslee identified them as being bandits. We were closing in behind them when we dropped our [external fuel] tanks, gave it the full boost and rapidly closed in. But they made a pass at the 2nd box getting strikes on several [B-17] Forts. They then kept going on through from the bombers' 10 o'clock to their 4 o'clock.
>
> We chased [one Messerschmitt 410, a heavy fighter] and the engagement took place from about 5,000 feet down to the deck. I made several passes at him observing strikes, and when I pulled away after one particular pass, I saw Lt. Emerson set [the 410's] starboard engine on fire.
>
> At this point Col. Blakeslee said to let him go, that he had "had it." But from where I was I could see he was running to get away so I closed in and clobbered him good getting strikes all around the cockpit. When I last saw

*him he was crash landing and burning badly. Then Col.
Blakeslee called me saying he had got the other one.*

*I joined up with him just as he was getting set for a
dead astern shot. I was to his starboard when he opened
fire clobbering him well, setting the underside of the 410 on
fire. [Col. Blakeslee] moved out and I came in and got in
a good burst at [the 410], then pulled away and watched
him try and crash land it – but it was burning worse than
ever and plowed into a woods, setting fire to the immediate
area around him.*

*I then joined up with Col. Blakeslee and we got to
about 5,000 feet when someone called in a Seaplane base
with about 15 Dol 8's on it. We made a wide orbit to port
and came in from south to north, Col. Blakeslee on the
port, I was to his right, Lt. Emerson to my right. I hit
two of these Seaplanes with good bursts. I did not hit the
same ones Col. Blakeslee did. I claim 1 Me 410 destroyed,
shared with Lt. Emerson and 2 Dol 8's damaged.*

The mission that day took a body-numbing six hours and thirty
minutes.

*Conrad's flight log was another holdover from the
RAF. Officially known as the Pilot's Flying Log Book,
Form 414, it came with a preprinted admonition: "This
book is an official document and is the property of His
Majesty's Government." After the war, these journals were
given to the flyers or their families.*

*Entries in Conrad's flight log would include an
unemotional catalogue of lost Allies. From May 9, 1944:
"lost four men including Sherman due to flak." From May
24: "Saw two forts get it over target – pretty sickening."
From May 25: "Red section got it – hard. Tom [McDill] and
Joe Bennett lost." From May 29: "Lost [Frank] Speer."*

Still other entries would register why he felt it was a great life. From
May 8, 1944: "Vapor trails making quite a sight." From May 21: "Fighter
sweep south of Berlin – ground strafing. Spent the most enjoyable 45
minutes in any airplane at any time." From May 27: "Saw the Alps off to
our right as we came into target area – beautiful. Saw Lake Constance
way off in the distance – gorgeous shade of blue." June 4: "Estuary of
Thames jam-packed with all sorts of shipping, barges, transports, etc."

Doing anything dumb or any exhibitionism was cause for punishment. Pat said that if he made a mistake, he "could have a stint 'on the flag' for a week. The flagman lines up the aircraft. Then when they are ready to go, the flagman waves them off. An important job, because a pilot can't see in front of him while on the ground. But, it was punishment, still." Conrad also worried about this. "It sure is easy to go right over this field and not see it. [But] there are so many other aerodromes about that there is no trouble at all to land, find out where you are, and then come on in." In this setting, Pat remembered the famous acronyms from the war. "We could have a snafu – situation normal, all fouled up. Or a tarfu – things are really fouled up. Or, the worst, fubar – fouled up beyond all recognition."

After a long show, Pat said that they did have time to relax. "We had a short-wave radio, and we could pick up anything on that thing. Usually, we would listen to Axis Sally because the music was good. We'd come back [from a show] and we'd be getting cleaned up or get ready to go to bed. We'd turn the radio on and listen to Axis. She had good music. She had Glenn Miller!"

The pilots could not take anything in their planes that would associate them or their plane with any unit. On the very real chance that the plane would go down, no one wanted to aid the enemy by carrying information helpful to them. The squadron's clerk-typist, Pickney "Pink" Lackey, gathered all of the pilots' personal items and then issued them an escape kit which included a compass, a photo of each pilot in civilian clothes (so La Résistance could make fake identity papers), and 500 French francs sealed in a waterproof wallet. These materials would be essential in helping a pilot downed in France escape to Spain. Once in Spain, he could return to Debden in a week or two.

While this kept the enemy from learning anything about the pilot, it kept the Allies from the same information. And this would prove detrimental to Conrad.

✳ ✳ ✳

Life was not so exciting for Katherine, nor for most of the young wives left behind to manage households, pregnancies, children, jobs, in-laws, finances, and emotions. During peacetime, they handled these elements of family life well, with help and companionship from their husbands, who were there to encourage, support, and, most of all, hold and caress them. The partnership worked both ways, with husbands needing the same from their wives. But during war, the couples had to use letters to convey what they would have said in person. The letters could not substitute for a hug and kiss, the gentlest touch, or the eyes locked in understanding. And without this, war was hell.

Mitigating that hell for Katherine were her pregnancy, her letters to Conrad, an occasional game of dominoes, and endless rounds of bridge with other ladies-in-waiting. The bridge games would migrate, when gas was available, from one home to another, with a hundredth-penny a point being the highest stakes allowed. Imagine the scene: four twenty-somethings, gabbing for hours, speculating on their pregnancies, playing mindless games of bridge, and, underneath it all, feeling unspeakably worried about their husbands' futures.

Katherine's letters reported newsy details of these comings and goings. She mentioned the dinners she cooked for the family: "meatloaf, glazed carrots, baked eggplant, frozen apple and Jell-O salad, rolls, and pie . . . and for $1.25." She fretted over finances: "I won't be able to save $100 this month as I had planned. But I'll soon have $800 saved in the baby fund." She reported on the baby: "Last Tuesday, the baby nearly kicked my appendix out. Since then, not a move." And she told of her various handyman projects: "I am going to build some shelves under the sink and drain board. We really need more space."

Katherine knew that whereas before, when he was in Texas, Conrad might have called, that was now impossible. Every problem, joy, and bit of news had to be handled by mail. "I write every day and mail the letters the same afternoon," she wrote in February. To post the letter, she walked five blocks to the drug store. Conrad wrote nearly every day, as well. With the post office delivering mail twice daily, the news rarely got old.

The military's version of special delivery, V-Mail, took a letter written on a bordered one-page form, photographed it using an early form of microfiche, reduced it, and sent it through the regular mail system. The intent was to produce smaller, lighter letters, thus saving valuable space and tonnage. Katherine and Conrad soon found that V-Mail was slower than normal mail, and used the latter exclusively thereafter. Either way, all mail from England was censored, though from their surviving letters that censoring does not appear to be heavy handed or even consistent.

They wrote about the topics every couple discusses, regardless of the circumstances:

Money. Conrad wrote: "I want to have plenty of cash in the bank when I get home. You don't realize it over there but from here it's quite plain to see that the fellow who has something to fall back on when this is all over is the man who will be able to stand on his feet when he gets back home." Katherine responded, "If you are gone a year – God forbid – I'll have $800 saved." She reminded him that the "March car payment is $36.10."

Faith in God. Conrad wrote, "You said you went to church – keep it up as much as you can. I don't as much as I'd like to, but you can help by going." Katherine responded, "I bless you every night, darling [in my prayers]. I pray for you many times every day."

Social life. He wrote: "Does Billie still call me a 'party boy'? I am, you know. Only now, I hook one arm over the Club bar and hang on. We had free beer again last night (fifteen or more destroyed on a show)." She wrote back: "We can't even work up a bridge game because everyone is out of gas. They are putting Texas on the same gasoline ration schedule as in the east. Two gallons a week on your A card, so my gasoline is going to be saved for the doctor and the laundry."

Shopping. Conrad wrote that he needed Prep, Pepsodent, Wildroot cream oil hair dressing, and, of course, gum. Katherine would search the Post Exchange at Fort Sam Houston, and many stores on Houston Street in San Antonio to find what he needed. Abiding by the strict standards for package sizes, she would pack the supplies to get the most to him in the least space. To keep packages to a minimum, the sender had to show the postal clerk the letter wherein the airman asked for the supplies. The clerk would then stamp the letter, thus restricting sending another package of the same supplies. Katherine shopped for herself, too. "I bought the first record I've bought since last July. 'I'll Be Seeing You.' It is lovely and I'll send you the words." This became their song.

Her family. Katherine wrote: "[Mama] is mighty fond of you, darling, and talks about her four boys in the service all the time.

Sometimes I have had to explain to people that she really just has three . . . but that doesn't stop her." Mrs. Henderson proudly displayed in her window a service flag consisting of a red border surrounding a white rectangle. Centered on the rectangle were four blue stars, one for each son in the service. Four-star service flags were rare, as Katherine confirmed in a letter to Conrad. "Mom at last found a service banner [at Joske's Department Store] with four stars on it. She has been hunting for some time without any success."

Worries. Conrad wrote, "In spite of all the 'glory stories' you read of fighter pilots, the only real glory as far as I'm concerned is getting back after each show, and that's just what I concentrate on. Amen." Katherine was no less worried. "O, I hate this war. Why couldn't we have lived another time? I'm so lonesome. I do hope the next time I see you will be for keeps, not this eternal separating." Later she wrote, "I wonder how many times I have read, 'Do not tell your soldier your troubles.' "

Convictions. "I [have] a characteristic that I sincerely hope will never change – certainly it hasn't changed yet. That is this: speak straight from the shoulder and expect everyone else to do the same; speak honestly and with the very weight of my honest convictions. I won't waver on that."

Future plans. Conrad wrote, "Tell you for sure, I don't want Conjon to be a fighter pilot. Think he'd make a much better goat rancher." Katherine had plans, too. "I'm so glad we are married. Think of all the marvelous years there are ahead. So many more than most people have. I know that our lives together are a perfect partnership – one that was created for a lifetime, not a few months. It is only at times that I resent your being taken from me, but, I'm so young yet – and so are you." Later she wrote:

> Gosh, darling, I miss not having all the fun so many other couples have had when they are married. I mean, that I'd not trade one minute of any time I've ever spent with you, but I do wish it could have been normally, like our folks and older friends had. Like just living in the same town, and having a wonderful time getting started housekeeping and having friends over for the first time in your own home, and all that. But perhaps it will be that we've had this much extra before we start on that.

*Perhaps we haven't missed a thing, but are on to a lot more
happiness than the ordinary couples are. Maybe when the
war is finally over and you've come home forever, it'll be
just like starting in for the first time. I'll like that, I know.
Gosh, if you knew all the things I plan for you and me
and Conjon, you'd know what I do with all my time. Just
daydream about you, that's all. And when you get home
at last! Well, there won't be a happier person in this world
than I will be. Nothing will spoil the rest of my life, after
you are here.*

Philosophy. He wrote, "Oh, if you all over there could only see
and listen to the British for *one hour*! That's all – then you'd see what's
called for when war is right at your front doorstep." She thought, on
paper: "Although I hate with every part of me the fact that you are
gone, I am still so proud to know that you were willing to do what
had to be done. . . . Another reason to add to the long, long list of why
I married you."

His job. He wrote: "None of us hold any kind of malice toward
the boys back home. Hell, some guys just don't want combat, that's
all. We asked for this, and wouldn't be happy without it. They didn't
and would only be a liability to the group over here. Remember this."
She encouraged him:

*Don't think you did wrong with your decision in
McAllen to go over. I'm glad you did, because I knew if I
asked you to stay, you would have. But I also knew that
you would never be quite satisfied with yourself, and what
you were doing. You've had wonderful opportunities and I
know it. You might have been stuck someplace where there
was just no place for me, teaching someone the art of Basic
Training. And I know you would have been miserable.*

*Now that I know you are gone, and that two months
have gone by, I know when you get back, we'll both be
completely satisfied that you've done everything you could
have done without any hesitation. So, don't regret taking
your chance to get over there. You've been so fortunate to get
such a swell place, and before Conjon is able to say, "CJN
IV," his daddy will be through and on his way home to us.*

And their child-to-be. Conrad's plans: "About my filling Conjon full of beautiful lies about my flying – well, he'll simply have to come with me when the 4th Fighter Group has a reunion – then we'll really know what it was all like here." Katherine, though, had the most time to think about her child, and to ruminate on what he (or, just possibly, she) would be like. She wrote:

> You can't tell now what he will grow up to look like, but I know what his mannerisms will be like. I could tell you right now how he'll stand when he's deep in conversation with someone. And how he'll walk like only one other person I've ever known walks. How his nails will look . . . . And his teeth, despite braces, will probably get too close together in a couple of places and he'll eventually have a package of dental floss in his pocket as much as he does gum, which he'll chew all the time.
>
> He'll grow up with a Time magazine under one arm and a model of a P-51 under the other. And he'll let his hair grow down on the left side instead of brushing it back. He'll have eyes that you can't quite decide the color of, sort of a cross between hazel and green and blue. And he'll be sort of hard to handle because he will definitely have a mind of his own. He'll fall for every pretty girl that walks along, until one day there arrives on the scene some girl he may have known all his life . . . He'll have enormous feet . . .
>
> And all the years that I can sneak in to look at him when he's asleep, he'll look like a little boy to me, and it'll be all I can do not to take him in my arms and hug him. He'll be too thin for years and then when he's married and has a few children, he'll start to take on a little weight and begin to get a little less anxious to be on the go. And above all, he'll be kind. He'll never be one of the boys that are mean to dogs . . . He will have a wonderful sense of humor, and the only thing he won't agree on with his daddy is that he will finally be grown and his own boss. Because his daddy will never realize it. His daddy will try for the rest of his life to sort of ease the bumps and steer the cart so there won't be any catastrophes. His shoulders will be

broad and we'll both worry because he's just sort of bow legged. And someday, he'll be the perfect husband to the second luckiest girl in the world. He'll be thoughtful, and gentle. And she'll be happy the rest of her life because he will be so fine and wonderful.

I suppose you know how I can tell you so much about him, even though he is still so tiny. It's because he's you, all over again. I can't do anything for you now, but write you every day and try to remind you of what a wonderful happiness we've had, and what a much more wonderful happiness for years to come we will have. So instead, I can take care of him. Because he is you. And the only thing he will inherit from me will be the love for his daddy.

CHAPTER EIGHT

———————— ★ ————————

A Fateful Strafing Run
Over Normandy, I

Conrad's work began well before sunup, depending on the weather and the show. Good weather was rare in that part of England; East Anglia could be socked in for days at a time. But when it cleared, the predawn, 5 a.m. assembly at Debden was a picture postcard. The P-51s would be ready for takeoff, more than a dozen of them weaving side-to-side so the pilots could see the plane in front. As the flagman waved each one into the cold morning mist, the sun's rays just bright enough for safety, the wheels retracted and the red-nosed silver planes with black markings were airborne, eager for their morning exercise. The young pilots were more than ready to give it to them. How confident they looked! Men and machines ready for the day's show.

The authoritative roar of the British-style Merlin engines – named by someone with a sense of England's mythic past – would power the air speed up to 250 m.p.h. so they could join the slower bombers, which would already be over the English Channel. As the rivulets of moisture drained back over the canopy and wings, the pilots settled in. The next four or five hours were what the planes were built for – air-to-air combat, killing, and destruction. But before all that, crossing the channel they looked like a syncopated airborne dance troupe, fully rehearsed, fully prepared, and ready for the opening curtain.

When not writing letters, Conrad was airborne and at war. The air battles over Europe were never more intense than in March and April 1944. To Katherine he wrote: "We had quite a time [on a show of 4:55 hours] what with flak and Jerry mixing us up a bit. And don't let anyone kid you – this flak is *no* joke. Had two close shaves [dodging enemy planes] and if they come any closer I'll know I didn't see it coming. It was a real, honest-to-goodness first look at the black cross painted on the airplane, and I'm not kidding myself into thinking I was a 'rock' among them – hell, I was scared stiff. And I will admit it twenty years from now, too." And to his parents: "I have one Jerry probably destroyed to my credit. I think my emotion at the time of firing and immediately after when I looked back of me to see if I had gotten him (he was coming straight at me) was one of almost complete composure and calm. [Through all this, Katherine] and the baby are constantly on my mind. I sure have hit it lucky all the way through." Composure and calm in the midst of battle would have gladdened the hearts of his training crew. He didn't go wobbly, didn't consider that someone died at his hands. He was ready; he was trained. At that moment, courage was not part of the equation.

Katherine was supportive: "I still can't get used to the idea of you over Germany actually fighting. I don't suppose I ever shall. I do admire your courage so much, and I wouldn't have one bit of you changed for anything in the world. It gives [me] the creeps to see all those black clouds just floating around and knowing the death that came up with them."

Though not frequently discussed, the flyers were obviously under emotional strain. Pat recalled: "Bomber crews spent hours in those planes on one show. I always thought they were [more heroic] than the fighter pilots. It was a harder physical job . . . How could you stand there and have somebody throw rocks at you and do nothing about it? Eventually they're going to hit you. That's why they went home after twenty-five missions." Later that limit was extended multiple times.

Also not discussed were the extremes between ground and air combat. Statistics show that between three and four ground soldiers were wounded for every one killed. The reverse was true in the air. On the ground more enlisted men were on the front lines than officers. Again, in the air it was the reverse. But for both, death was brutal and violent.

The men frequently talked about how long they would be overseas. Even before the invasion, which everyone knew was coming, what could they expect? "You should be home in about nine months. And completely covered with ribbons" was one unconfirmed report. Conrad wrote his brother Bob, "I have twenty-one hours toward the 200 for one tour after which we all sign up for another, like it or not." As his operations hours mounted, he welcomed the Army's acknowledgment. "That eighty-two hours [of operations time] entitles me to the first cluster to my Air Medal." But he had a long road ahead. He would have to endure the combat days that were left, however many, with controlled anxiety. He wrote Katherine: "About the number of missions, I can tell you this for sure – we'll be here until the war in Europe is over. And that's all there is to it. It's all on official order and there's nothing more I can say about it. This old '200 hours and you're home' doesn't go anymore for us." It got worse. "A tour is no longer 200 hours. Now 300 hours." And worse. After May 1944, the tour hours were unlimited.

Slowly, the number of hours and shows mounted. "We're having a party Sunday night celebrating over 500 victories – World's record. Our 200 [shows] this month are likewise a record. We're hot!"

One day, though, it was Conrad who was hot – under the collar. He wrote Katherine: "Something has just happened that has made me sick. We have a new guy flying with us and on his first time up on a practice flight with some of the boys, what does he do but prang *my* kite in landing it! Damn it. My chief and I have nursed and babied it ever since we got it and then he does a thing like that – 100 percent pilot error and has the nerve and audacity to blame it on 'brake lock.' Oh, I tell you, we're hopping mad and the C.O. knows it – knows the guy is no good. Damn!"

Though Conrad was to get a new kite, probably a newer P-51, a model D, it apparently never

Lt. Conrad John Netting III in May 1944 in front of his P-51, named Conjon IV in the expectation that his new child would be a boy. In the background are two wing tanks to carry the extra fuel needed to make it from England's Debden Airfield to Berlin and back.

arrived, which might have suited him just fine. Most pilots preferred the more maneuverable model B. So he sent a picture of himself and his P-51B home to Katherine. "[I want to send you a picture] of Conjon IV which looks not too bad considering it was pranged and then patched up. I had my picture taken in front of *the* kite today. Of course, I needed a shave. And won't *that* look nice, now." To his parents he wrote about the same picture: "The name Conjon IV is simply that it had better be Conrad John Netting IV in July or I rename my kite. The item in the background is one of the two external wing tanks we carry making possible our Berlin shows."

Illustrated London News reported: "Because [the 4th Fighter Group] is such a crack group, they have been given the most difficult of all fighter operations – a battle that requires great physical endurance, extreme fighting skill and tremendous courage. To fly and fight for five or six hours on end." Dignitaries throughout England, both political and military, often delivered their praise in person. Conrad wrote to Katherine: "The biggest news we've had in many a moon is about the visit we had today [April 11, 1944] – more generals all together in one room than I'd ever seen individually before. There was, to name the ones you'd recognize, quite a bevy – Eisenhower, Spaatz, Doolittle . . . I was down front and could of easily patted Ike or Doolittle on the head."

This visit by Eisenhower was reported in *The New York Times*: "Fourth Fighter Group pilots were told today by General Eisenhower that their role in the great three-way invasion of Europe soon would be that of flying a dawn-to-dusk death express against the German Air Force. . . . General Eisenhower said he had a feeling of great privilege and almost humility in visiting such a group of fighting men as the Fourth." Eleanor Roosevelt visited as well. These luminaries weren't at Debden for the awards alone. Its reputation for the best food and the best parties was the cause for many visits. The dignitaries often flew in, resulting in assorted aircraft, both British and American, moored on the tarmac. Headlining one party was the famous chorus of London's Windmill Theater.

After the parties and the dignitaries, the flyboys went back to work, knowing that within days the intensity would increase with Operation Overlord. The project was no secret, as equipment blanketed every flat surface of southeast England. The question was when? To maintain security, as much routine was followed at Debden as possible. Flights over France were more frequent, but that didn't reveal the date and time. To keep matters completely normal, even passes were distributed.

"I got a forty-eight-hour pass this morning and here I sit writing you. Am planning on going in [to Cambridge] and play golf with my crew chief and Tom's old chief. They are great buddies. Then I guess we'll hit Cambridge for supper." The letter's date was June 5, 1944. That afternoon, back at Debden, an order was received to paint all planes with eighteen-inch bands, alternating black and white, the distinguishing markings for the D-Day invasion.

* * *

D-Day is the most ambitious military effort in U.S. military history: 175,000 Allied troops, 6,000 warships, and 12,000 planes. No other military campaign has come close, and the Eighth Air Force was integral to the effort. According to *1000 Destroyed*: "Eighth Air Force fighters were assigned on D-Day to form a wall south, east, and west of the beachhead to prevent Luftwaffe craft from penetrating to the beachhead. The 4th Fighter Group's assignment was to sweep the area around Rouen, France." Against those, 12,000 aircraft poised for the invasion. Germany had less than 300.

Katherine, of course, had heard all about the invasion. She wrote on June 6: "At last it has happened. I've been listening to all the reports today over the radio and it seems that the Allies are holding their own. Perhaps now the Allies will be able to end the European war before long. I feel so sorry for the poor boys that will be killed during these first terrible days. I don't suppose I shall ever reconcile myself to war and all the horrors of it, as little as I know of it. But I shall never understand why the waste and destruction is allowed. Darling, be careful and take very good care of yourself for me, please. I can't do without you."

Conrad wrote on June 9 to Katherine: "War is certainly no excuse for finding the 'right' kind of government. The damage has been terrible not only there but here in England, also. Since the invasion started two days ago, we've been going at a faster clip than ever. But with *no* opposition!" That same day she wrote: "I sometimes think it is harder on the mothers than the wives, because mothers are older, and they watched that boy grow from nothing to a man. Even though a wife's whole life is gone, she, being younger, seems to me to be able to take it better than a mother, who as you put it 'dotes' on her son. It is sheer tragedy any way you look at it." Dwight D. Eisenhower felt the same: "I hate war as only a soldier who has lived it can, only as one who has seen its brutality and stupidity."

Conrad's family wrote often. His father wrote, "My hearty and best wishes for your success, and may our Heavenly Father guide and direct on all your trips. [We wish that you] too will soon experience the Love of God expressed in terms of the greatest gift any two people can experience – a perfect baby. God bless and keep you this day and for many days to come. 'O Saviour of the world, who by thy Cross and precious Blood hast redeemed us, save us and help us, we humbly beseech Thee, O Lord.' "

Though his father's letters reflected prayers of confidence, Conrad Jr. later carried with him a prayer that was more pragmatic:

> Protect him, God, wherever he may be,
> And guide him safely through the bitter night
> That shrouds the bloody fields of Normandy,
> Where tortured youth press onward with the fight.
> Have mercy on him, God, and bring him back.
> But should his hour come, as it may,
> Should fate write finis to his valiant quest,
> Let him go out locked in the heat of the fray,
> Then grant his weary soul eternal rest.
>
> – *Martin F. Owen*

And from his mother: "[On D-Day,] never have I known so many people to say they went to church or that they had read the President's prayer." Franklin Roosevelt's prayer supporting Operation Overlord was this:

> Almighty God: Our sons, pride of our nation, this day have set upon a mighty endeavor, a struggle to preserve our republic, our religion, and our civilization.

They will be sore tried, by night and by day, without rest – until the victory is won. Some will never return. Embrace these, Father, and receive them, thy heroic servants, into thy kingdom.

Conrad's grandmother wrote: "[Your Bible verse is,] 'He shall call upon me, and I will answer him, I will be with him, I *will deliver* him.' Psalm 91:15. So be not afraid, only believe" [her emphasis]. The 91st Psalm was a common one for the men to read before battle. "Fears must vanish as the dew in the morning sun."

She might also have quoted Psalm 46, which reverberated in many hearts and on the lips of countless worshipers: "God is our refuge and strength, a very present help in trouble." Or the words spoken to Joshua: "I will not fail thee nor forsake thee."

Seeing no serious resistance from the Luftwaffe just after D-Day, the mission of the 4th Fighter Group was modified from air-to-air combat defending the bombers to air-to-ground combat defending the foot soldiers and their equipment. Targets on the ground might include convoys, railroad lines, bridges, aircraft factories, airfields, radio installations, and, of course, Germans. Though this decision was essential, it made the P-51 into something it was not and that had not been dreamed of when it was designed.

From *Deadly Sky*: "If the prospect of dog fighting provoked elation and excitement among pilots, then strafing usually evoked the opposite. It was deadly, dangerous business because missions were flown at such low altitudes. But such close air support proved the most effective use of airpower in World War II. Allied fighters shot up trains, trucks, tanks, bunkers, communications centers, soldiers, and many other targets. Strafing, not dog fighting, presented the greatest danger to the pilot."

"Strafing" comes from the German word *strafe*, a verb meaning to punish, which the Germans used when they invented the procedure thirty years before. The *Mighty Eighth War Manual* explains:

Strafing was a German term adopted by the Allies to describe aircraft shooting up the enemy on the ground. The salient points were approach the target at medium altitude; let down when far enough away so as to be unobserved and to avoid alerting the defenses;

fly at tree-top height for a few miles before reaching the target so as to achieve surprise; make only one line abreast pass to keep losses to a minimum. After attacking, aircraft continued to fly low, under fifty feet if possible, for some distance, avoiding any area that might be defended when climbing back to high altitude. Despite these precautions losses to ground strafers rose steadily during the final nine months of the war and opportunity strafing was banned by the beginning of 1945.

Conrad had been adept at this low-level flying even in his early solo training. He enjoyed it, showing the special coordination it took to pull it off. Did his marginal eyesight help or hurt? The answer is unknown. He wrote Randall on June 9, "We have been doing a lot of strafing and glide and skip bombing with excellent results." The strafing would continue, though it was not what most of the pilots ever thought they would be doing. They dreaded the strafing because the underbelly of the P-51, and its vulnerable air-cooling system, were exposed to small arms fire. Once hit at twenty or thirty feet of altitude, you had no chance to bail out. You were in the plane no matter what.

On June 9, Conrad wrote Katherine, "Of twenty-one [men] who came here together [on April 4], ten are gone."

"During the days just after D-Day, every thirty seconds two more aircraft commenced their runs together as element leader and wingman," Pat recalled. These designations for the pilots revealed the hierarchy involved on each mission. The section leader, the most skilled pilot, was designated no. 1 with his wingman as no. 2. The element leader, or hunter, was no. 3. His wingman was no. 4. Thus, four planes were involved in each tactical section. The wingman protected his leader from being attacked from the rear; he had a critical and exclusively defensive role.

On June 10, Conrad and Pat were just two of many flying toward France in formation like mechanized geese. The 4th Fighter Group's mission had changed to comport with the realities of the D-Day invasion. First, with the Luftwaffe's fighters outnumbered eight to one by the Allied planes, the enemy could mount no sustained air-to-air combat. This left the Allies, and the 4th Fighter Group in particular, to fly interdictory missions, emphasizing targets of opportunity.

Thousands of feet above Normandy, above the heroic ground troops, Pat's assignment was to strafe enemy resources. Find 'em, strafe 'em, and be back for lunch. With no Luftwaffe evident, this was a milk run. Down below he could see the fields in every shade of green, dairy cattle fenced in by hedgerows grown impenetrable over the centuries. His squadron included his best friend and roommate, Conrad, his senior by four years, and thus an old man at twenty-six. As they cruised for targets of opportunity, they talked on the A button of their radios. Conrad noticed a three-truck German convoy along a country road. No problem. Con said he'd take the lead. Pat would become his wingman – his right-hand man and protector. Routine. Just keep the leader alive; watch his back. That was the wingman's job. With no enemy planes anywhere, what could go wrong?

Pat recalled: "We were returning from an escort mission. And somebody [identified] this [German] convoy and to come help them. Conrad was to my right. He was furthest to the right, so he went in first. I followed him on down. And obviously in a hilly region, they're going to run roads in the valleys. So when we went down on [the convoy], there was another hill on the other side. So when he went down on it, he paid more attention to his strafing than he did to what was coming up. And when he turned up, there wasn't enough room." The high-reaching trees on the hillside were more than a match for the plane. The French records would later verify: "As he started to lift the nose of his plane to gain altitude, the pilot's aircraft began spiraling downward and plunged toward the ground south of the 'Pont Hardy' farm. The crash was caused by a sudden loss of speed, not by enemy gunfire."

What happened between his strafing and when he turned up? We'll never know, but "target fixation," an ominous military phrase, is a possibility. The Navy League describes it thus: "The mountainous terrain was another obstacle. . . . [O]ur pilots had to be constantly alert to the topography. There also was a danger that, in bombing or strafing runs, paying too much attention to the target could result in flying into a mountain while pulling out of a dive."

The summary Conrad had written in his combat report a few weeks before now applied to him: he "plowed into a woods, setting fire to the immediate area around him."

* * *

In the control tower diary, the entry at 11:22 a.m. reported that all pilots eventually returned unharmed except Netting, Becky 61, VF-S. "No contact with him. Squadron reports one of the aircraft was seen to go down." By 5 p.m. on June 10, 1944, the diary shows Netting killed in action.

That evening, Pat wrote in Conrad's flight log:

> *Today's was Con's last flight. He flew as an extra, and in his eagerness to stop an enemy truck convoy from reaching the beachhead, he gave his life. Con was going in on a truck, leading the rest of the squadron to it, and while he was firing, he got too close and when he pulled up, his ship hit the trees, turning it over and it was seen to crash and explode.*
>
> *I lost a very good friend today and the squadron will miss him as a valuable man – but it will be nothing as compared to the loss to Katherine and Conjon IV.*

CHAPTER NINE

★

Conjon IV – "The Largest Baby" – and Two Telegrams

Before word reached San Antonio, Katherine, eight months pregnant, continued to write her daily letters. "I really hate to read in your letters about the boys who are down. It is really terrible. And yet, you know, even though I read about those other boys, I know I'll never read that about you. Do you suppose it is woman's intuition or something? I just *know* it. Wait and see if I'm not right. Never feel alone, darling, because you're not. Ever. I'm always with you. Can you feel it?" Conrad never got those letters.

On June 23, 1944, the dreaded telegram arrived, its message conveyed in Western Union's cold, unbroken capital letters.

> THE SECRETARY OF WAR DESIRES ME TO EXPRESS HIS DEEP REGRET THAT YOUR HUSBAND SECOND LIEUTENANT CONRAD J. NETTING HAS BEEN REPORTED MISSING IN ACTION SINCE TEN JUNE OVER FRANCE IF FURTHER DETAILS OR OTHER INFORMATION ARE RECEIVED YOU WILL BE PROMPTLY NOTIFIED
> = ULIO THE ADJUTANT GENERAL

On June 26 Katherine began a journal that she kept for over six months, until she learned for certain her husband was dead. She began with her logic. "You may never read this, my darling, but I'm writing it because I want in some way to tell you all of the things that have happened since I got word of your being missing. If you are well and safe now, this will be an interesting thing for you to read some day. But if, God forbid, you are dead, this will at least be a way for me to tell you, wherever you are now, what the last few days have been like, and what the rest will be like."

If it had been today, Katherine would attend support groups and see counselors, all for the worthwhile purpose of helping her sort through her feelings. In 1944, such steps were inconceivable, leaving her and the other war widows to their own devices. And the core device she chose was keeping a journal.

Her first entry recounted receiving the telegram.

> I had just brought the paper into Grannie and I noticed the date – June 23, 1944 . . . Friday. I'll never forget that date as long as I live. I was lying on the bed . . . and I got to thinking about you to bring you closer to me. I also thought of what I would do if I ever got a telegram that you were hurt or killed or missing. It isn't strange that I should be thinking such a thing just before I heard those fateful steps on the porch, because, I can tell you now, that there was never a day that passed that I haven't wondered just how long it would be before I heard.
>
> I was totally unprepared for it this time, though, because I had had letters from you for two days in a row. And, I had a feeling that once you got through the fighting of the invasion, you would be all right. Funny how your mind plays tricks on you so you can be at peace, a little bit, anyway.
>
> But somehow I did know when I heard those very slow steps what it was. I couldn't get to the door at all, it seemed. And when the man asked me, "Mrs. Katherine H. Netting?" I knew for sure what I was about to read. I took the book and very carefully signed Mrs. K. H. Netting someplace. I'm sure I don't know where, but he handed the wire to me. I turned away from the door and tore open the envelope very carefully. And I didn't read it. I just looked to see "Conrad J. Netting" "Missing" "France" "10 June."
>
> I think I sat in the large chair then, but I'm not sure. I wandered around the room aimlessly for a few minutes. There were several times when a tear would seep out, but I never cried. Then I walked back to Grannie's room and I noticed, as though I weren't myself, but a third person watching myself in a dream, that I was shaking terribly . . .

I can't think of you as any way but alive. And if they ever do finally tell me that you aren't I shall never be able to accept it. I shall never be able to remember you as anything but the most vivid, alive person I've ever known. They could even show me pictures to prove it, and I will never believe it. It will be my cross, my curse, and my joy forever, that in my mind, you shall always be vibrantly alive as you were when I had you with me.

I'm tired now, my darling, so I shall stop for this night.

Katherine quickly telegrammed Conrad's parents, who were living in Seattle on government assignment. From there word spread to other relatives and friends. Then she went about the most mechanical tasks: she painted the base to the backyard swing, iced a cake, fixed supper, cleaned the yard, mailed letters. And still she hadn't cried. Finally, after supper, "I sat on Mom's lap and a few of the millions of unshed tears fell."

Katherine wrote in her journal regularly, expressing all the feelings that she couldn't or wouldn't say. In late June she wrote, convinced that Conrad would return, "Now that I'm up-to-date on these letters that will never be mailed, I'll try to keep up. Because when (notice how my subconscious mind keeps putting you in the future?) you come, I want you to know all the little things that have happened to me. That way we'll be much closer." And, "I just can't seem to last the darkness out." Then she wrote, mentioning their song, "If I ever learn you are not to return to me in this world, I'll know somewhere you are waiting for me. I'll be seeing you."

Missing in action was frequently assumed by the military because in the heat of combat death was often not certain. Further, if a soldier was missing in action his full pay, allowances, and allotments continued. If he was declared dead they stopped. Despite its financial advantage, the designation left open the possibility that the serviceman was alive, and families would cling to this for months while the military worked out the facts.

By the end of June Katherine feared the worst. "If I hear you have died, or that you are still 'missing,' I shall go to work leaving the baby in Mom's care. I know very well that even if you are dead (oh, my

"Missing" was written by a military postal officer on the envelope of a letter returned to Katherine Netting on June 14, 1944. Her husband's plane had crashed in Normandy four days earlier, and his fate was still officially undetermined.

God, what it costs to write that), I would be taken care of the rest of my life by our combined families, if I let them. But your baby is my responsibility and yours. And if God has left it all in my hands, I will not shirk it. So as soon as I can, I shall begin to work, so that I might bring your child up as best I can."

The journal entries continued into July, each bringing some added consolation. Katherine wrote: "I suppose it is a very foolish, and mentally unhealthy thing I'm doing now. I mean, writing you. I have heard it isn't good for one to dwell on things, but I've noticed that when I write you all the things, good and bad, that have happened to me during the day, I feel much easier. It helps me forget some of the sadness when I write it out. I can't think of you after June 10. I don't know how. My mind goes from agonizing pictures of you dead in your plane, to ones of you as a PW [prisoner of war], but neither seems real." Sad reminders kept coming. "I got a letter from [Headquarters, Army Air Force] telling me you were last seen near Evreux, France, 10:00 AM, bombing mission, June 10, 1944. Nothing else is known about the 'disappearance of Lt. Netting's aircraft.' Oh, my darling, where are you?"

* * *

Less than a month after that telegram arrived so did I, Conrad John Netting IV. Early in the morning of July 16, 1944, at the Fort Sam Houston hospital in San Antonio came the fifth-generation Conrad. Later that day, my mother wrote my father in her journal:

> *Yes, my darling, Conjon came this morning at 5:50 ayem – O, Conrad, he is so much your son. His little nose is an exact duplicate of the one you arrived with according to your baby pictures. His hairline is the same and he has BIG feet and hands. They say at the hospital that he is the largest baby delivered that the night nurse ever saw – NINE POUNDS 4 OZ. . . . I got to hold him this morning, and he is the spitting image of you. If only I knew you were safe. How happy I would be. Thank you my darling for your son. I love you.*

The emotional swings my mother was experiencing must have been nearly unbearable. In a journal entry the next day, July 17, their first wedding anniversary, she wrote, "Today has been anything but dull." Then, in the next paragraph, "I'm glad today has been so busy." Finally, in the close she wrote, "I'm terribly lonesome." Adding to her melancholy was seeing other women in the maternity ward who would "talk about their husbands all day, and then they come out at visiting hours. Gosh, I wish you were here." How could she have possibly coped with that isolation?

She wrote on July 18: "A year and a day [since their wedding]. We've done a lot of living in such a short time, and I want about 65 more years." She, of course, was clinging to the hope that Conrad was alive. This hope added to her moodiness during pregnancy and further extended her emotions postpartum. Also, her three brothers were in the military, though none in a forward position. And she was taking home a baby, born of a love she thought she could never have, who would not know a father. "I cry until I can't cry another tear."

Her room at home was barely big enough for a bed and dresser, and in that confining space she would have to live with her baby. The clapboard house, built in the early 1920s, was far too small for four generations. But this was her home, and in this room she had been born; this was where she would make it. With her husband in the war, what choice did she have other than to live with her mother, father – when he was at home – and grandmother? And what would happen when her two unmarried brothers came home from the war? Six adults and a baby? Well, she'd think about that later. For now, think only of today, of the gift and loss of life.

Pat Patteeuw, of course, had no doubt that Conrad was dead. His squadron and group knew as well. A quartermaster was assigned to remove Conrad's possessions from his room. In the Eighth Air Force, with casualties alarmingly high, this was a full-time job. Within a day or two, Pat recalled: "[The quartermaster] probably made arrangements with me and went up to the room with me and said, 'What's Conrad's and what's yours?' And I would tell them, 'this, this, and this,' and they'd just throw it all in the footlocker. And they must have asked *me* because I would be the only one that would know."

He saw the crash and explosion and knew Conrad couldn't have lived through it. So confident was he, and so motivated to put Katherine's mind at rest, that on July 9 he wrote Katherine:

> *You asked for whatever news I could tell you, and I'm afraid it's all bad. . . . His ship crashed and he never got out of it. . . . I took care of all of his belongings. . . . As long as this war must cost men, I wish it could be men like myself who have no families or anyone close to them. I guess there is a higher Being who must decide these things.*

Conrad's parents, seeking more information, wrote to their son's commanding officer, who apparently asked Pat Patteeuw to respond. His letter of July 25 was honest and blunt.

> *I am sorry I cannot give you any encouragement, sir, for knowing Con as well as I did I should be more than happy if I could. Con's accident came about while strafing a convoy of trucks, and in his eagerness to do the job perfectly he crashed into the ground. . . . This war has taken the lives of many wonderful people, and will undoubtedly take many more, but that is our price to preserve all the things which we hold so dear.*

These two letters began Katherine's slow acknowledgment of reality. She wrote on August 7 in her journal:

> *Dearest Conrad,*
>
> *The bad news has come. On the fifth, Saturday, I received a letter from your father quoting a letter from Pat saying you are dead. Then, Mom showed me one Pat wrote me that was received the day Bob [Conrad's brother] arrived [July 20]. They (Mom, Dad, and Bob) decided not to show it to me while I was still so weak [from the pregnancy and birth]. But, of course, since I had the letter from your father it doesn't matter. So, you crashed into a truck convoy. Why did it have to be you? I know what my destiny is now.*

Pat recalled that Katherine wrote him a scathing letter suggesting he keep out of her business, and how dare he say Conrad was dead when nothing yet was certain. Pat recalled, "The timing was bad. It couldn't have been worse. Her denial was absolutely complete." In October 1944, she wrote to Conrad's parents, "[The War Department] at least did not verify Pat's story. I have written Pat several weeks ago requesting all details. If he writes with certainty that no mistake is possible, I shall communicate with the [War Department]."

Pat responded with the same certainty of his earlier letters.

> *Con was flying right next to one of the other boys when he saw this German convoy of trucks and tanks. He called them out on the radio to the rest of us, and he was the first one to go down, with this other fellow right behind him. He strafed the truck, but held his dive too long, and when he pulled out sharply he hit the top of the trees. His ship snapped over onto its back and then crashed and exploded into the ground. The fellow flying with him saw the whole thing. I was about a mile from there, strafing another part of the same convoy, so I didn't see it myself. There can be no doubt that it was Con's ship as he was the only one missing that day.*

Pat never contacted Katherine again, and she never mentioned him, trying, still, to deny Conrad's death and blaming the messenger for the message. Their aborted relationship was another casualty of war.

For the rest of 1944, Pat had five roommates over six months. "They're all gone. They didn't come back. I don't know what happened. See, after Conrad went down, I wasn't keen on – I – I don't even know their names. Deliberately. I was afraid of getting too close because this hurt enough already. And I didn't want it to happen again. Some didn't even last two weeks. [One that I trained] was there two days, and he's gone. [That feeling of separateness] lasts for about sixty years. Not getting close to anybody. I don't want to be hurt anymore."

His torment, still just below the surface after six decades, must have led him to wonder if he had let those men down, killed them just as surely as the Germans did, through imperfect training, a bad decision, or poor flying. Whatever the reason, they were gone and he was not. He was alive but filled with bitterness and survivor's remorse.

Pat said: "There was no ending to [being stationed] overseas. And I was completely shocked when somebody called me and told me [I was going home]. I had a hard time getting my mind – because *nobody* went home. Nobody *ever* went home. You just stayed there until one day you didn't come back. But *I* went home! And I looked around, and I said, 'Why not Conrad? He has a wife back there. I have no one, absolutely nobody. I don't have a girlfriend. I don't have any parent. I don't have anybody.' And I kept looking around the room . . ."

Condolences for Katherine arrived from friends, but they held guarded wording because of Conrad's MIA status. Conrad's mother wrote a friend, "Katherine . . . [is] just as dear to us as our own daughter would be and we will do anything we can to make things a bit easier for her." With the same spirit, Conrad's grandmother wrote: "I have not given up hope yet that Connie is still alive, and if he has passed on, I am sure it must be for the best of all, as God never makes a mistake, and some day we shall know *why*. We miss Connie more than ever. He always was so kind and thoughtful of Dad and me, and always smiling when he came home. We received such a lovely letter from Katherine a couple of weeks ago. She is a brave girl these trying days."

By August, some friends were acknowledging that Conrad had died, though his death was still not officially registered. A close friend eloquently wrote:

> [We appreciate] the supreme sacrifice that Connie has [made]. [He] had finished his earthly work in an honorable and just way for he was a good lad, and who had not only improved his time by labor but had great respect for his parents also his supreme parent, God.
>
> He has not gone from us for there is no separation or death in God's kingdom. He has advanced to a higher and better sphere of action where he will accomplish much more than he did in his earthly realm.
>
> I hope that you may see him as Ada and I do, that is as God's idea in the image and likeness of God and as such forever continuing on to better things.
>
> For your solace you must place yourselves along side of many thousands having the same experience and with faces lifted up to heaven, praise God for the wonderful accomplishments resulting from these sacrifices. By these Conjon will be protected.

Bob Netting, Conrad's younger brother, now in the Navy, wrote to Conrad's unit asking for more facts. The response came from Lt. Donald Emerson, who, on the day Conrad crashed, was the Becky Blue section leader flying in the squadron with Conrad. In it he wrote, "What happened was . . . just one of those things that happens to the best of us. I'm giving it straight from the shoulder – there is no hope." Bob probably kept these comments to himself.

Months passed. Katherine's uncertainty was agonizing, softened only by the round-the-clock distraction of a baby in the house and by her journal. The other women in the house doted on me, allowing my mother reflective time that brought with it a gut-wrenching melancholy.

> Shakespeare wrote, "Your love remembered, such joy brings; I would not change my place with kings."
>
> Oh, gosh, darling, I think I'm wearing all these memories thin. I've remembered and remembered and

remembered all the things we did together in Texas and in Florida and in New Orleans and on the train to there. And I'm going to need some new memories soon. So, take care of yourself, and hurry home. I love you with all my heart.

Gradually, she began to imagine that Conrad might have died.

I wish I knew if you are alive or not. If you are, how unbounded my joy shall be. If you aren't, I'd like to know if you know of our doings. I know you are in heaven if you are dead, so I know I must do everything in my power to join you there when my time comes. It would help a lot to know that you know all about Conjon and me, as we go along without you. I wish I could know about you. But I suppose that is heaven, isn't it, knowing what the person you love most is doing – and it will be my heaven if ever in this world or another we are reunited and know that it is for always.

I have grown older, faster, than anyone. I'm so lonesome for you. The endless years stretching ahead are almost too stark to face. Too bad you are gone. I'm lonely. Tonight I feel so confident that you are all right . . . I'm waiting for the time we'll meet again. It can't be too long, but I can wait forever. Will there ever come a time when I can think of you with no pain, only a pleasant glow or a lovely memory? Oh, darling, don't just be a memory. Be a future, not a past. Come home to me.

By autumn Katherine's journal entries began to tilt resignedly to Conrad's death.

You [have been missing] almost 4 [months]. It seems an eternity – yet a moment, I am so confused. I'm not sad, exactly – more wistful. I'm learning memories don't fade; they grow more brilliant – as does my love.

Someday we'll meet again. I'm waiting for our real life to begin. I can wait forever.

Someday we will know how perfect our life can be without fear of separation. It is a cheering thought that you are waiting for me – only a little piece away – waiting to take my hand and lead me to a paradise I can only dream

of. If that paradise is here or beyond, don't tire of waiting.
I'll be with you soon.

Katherine, on occasion, wrote for the thousands of wives who were wondering if their husbands were truly just missing in action. Her words spoke for those she would never meet.

You, if you are dead, are immortal to God as I may someday be. The beauty of our love is too God-sent to perish in mortal life. God will bring our interlude of separation to an end – whether in months or years – and finally our love will grow without impediment. I'm as a musical instrument, untuned before our love, able only to make discordant sounds, ready now to give faith all I possess in emotion because I am your beloved.

I feel very calm tonight. Waiting is not without some satisfaction, for as I wait, I know how I shall rejoice if you come home. And if I am to hear you have gone to your true home, I shall be more peaceful for having had months to realize my good fortune in having known you.

Conjon will be a living memorial to you, but he will also be a living hope for his children.

I love you, darling, peacefully, deeply, gratefully.

In late November, Katherine received word from the War Department that, in addition to the Purple Heart, Conrad had been awarded the Air Medal with two bronze Oak Leaf Clusters for "exceptionally meritorious service in aerial flight over enemy occupied Continental Europe. The courage, coolness and skill displayed by this Officer reflect great credit upon himself and the Armed Forces of the United States." Though they had still not declared Conrad dead, the letter continued, as only a committee-written letter could, that the awards "cannot be formally presented to your husband at this time," a deft way of avoiding the issue. To further frustrate the reader, the brigadier general who wrote the letter added, "May I again express my deepest sympathy." "No, you may not," Katherine might well have said, "because you have not yet declared my husband dead."

Katherine forwarded a copy of the letter to Conrad's parents and grandparents, adding her thoughts: "This shows that Conrad was doing all he could and more. Conjon will really have a father to live up to. Our son, grandson, and husband has done all he could – and courageously."

She continued in another letter to Conrad's parents: "We are fortunate for having had Conrad for as long as we did. Don't feel sorry about anything. We will never know what he would want us to do because he thought he would come home. Still, we can know from his joy of living that he would want us to go on as best we can without him. Remember that Conrad was only a mortal but he died in a glorious way – doing his part for us all and above all for his son. We have so many blessings, never stop counting them."

After receiving the letter about the medals, she wrote these poems.

Missing in Action

On flame-seared foreign field in France
My heart may now be sleeping.
The joys and sorrows of fickle chance
Deep in my soul are ever steeping.

From hours exquisite together sown
The grain of pain I'm reaping.
Without, sustained by love once known
Within, I'm ever weeping, weeping.

Air Medal

For courage, skill, and coolness in a creditable way
My love has given all he had. Come is my night, gone is my day.

I never wanted medals just to prove his noble worth.
I've always known, because I've loved him from the first.
Will that be all I'll ever have to show our son someday?
No, I can tell him more by far than citations ever say.

I can tell him of his goodness, of his kindness and his pride
Of being what he was – a man – honest and brave. Beside
the things they write about there is so much to know.
I shall spend my life reviewing his, so our son will like him grow.

Even a radio program could transform reverie into reality. A popular song in December 1944 was "Put Another Chair at the Table," sung by the Mills Brothers. Imagine hearing these words knowing that your own husband probably would never come back: "But now I'm coming home to you, my dear. The time will soon be here. . . . So, put another chair at the table. Put another chair there for me."

And still no official word from the government. Katherine was grasping for straws, trying to put form to a formless plight. Looking for logic, she wrote, "Your father thinks I don't hear [if you are alive] because you are so destroyed – materially – that there is nothing."

On New Year's Eve 1944, Katherine resolved to control her life better in the coming year.

> *I have decided to grow up. I think I have faced this tragedy very well so far. But in the future, I plan to really be an adult woman, conscious of my responsibilities and my blessings. I have been thinking: I am so fortunate to have had you, and doubly so now that I have Conrad IV. So, I will discipline myself and refuse to make a sad thing of our life together. I intended to be stronger where I was inclined to be weak. But in the future, I shall try to hold myself from all bitterness when I am inclined toward it. I shall stop coveting what others have. I shall be more thankful for what I have.*
>
> *I will look for one of two things in 1945. Either I shall have good news or I shall have bad. Of the 365 days ahead, surely one will be "it." If I learn you are dead – why, I shall know that the worst has happened, and I shall feel that from the worst there is only one path – to the best.*
>
> *So you see, I am not content, more resigned, and I am still praying for you, my darling, my darling. I love you.*

In January 1945, the condolences continued. Conrad's former supervisor, who had not seen Conrad for over two years, wrote to Conrad's parents:

> *Anything which any of us might say is inadequate but the knowledge that others are wanting to share your grief and are praying that mothers and fathers will have the*

courage and strength to carry on may be of some help. Our company is not unmindful of the high price which is being paid in the fight for freedom, and that Con's friends and co-workers will cherish his memory.

One of those co-workers wrote to Katherine:

Your husband was a loyal and valued member of this organization. He was respected and liked by his fellows. All of us will miss him and we can do no less than promise to carry on as he would want us to. You have our deepest sympathy. We share in your grief and in the pride felt by those whose loved ones have done well before they go to their rest . . . as Lincoln said, "Have laid so costly a sacrifice on the altar of freedom."

And much later, from someone who did not know Conrad nor any of this family, but knew of what he did: "One may imagine the wartime nobility only those in combat really understand, but how could anyone know what it must be like to write those letters knowing each could be the last? Now *there* is character! I suspect he pictured his young bride and without regret or despair because in the end he knew the righteous cause for which he died and to die as such in battle is to be forever young."

Decades later, Conrad's college friend Ross Novelli Sr. wrote: "How fondly I remember him. A great guy, always happy and cheerful with a smile such as shown [in front of his plane], but in person, more so. [He] was a great man and I thank God I knew him."

On January 8, 1945, almost exactly seven months after the crash, the government officially declared Conrad killed in action and telegraphed his widow.

REPORT NOW RECEIVED FROM THE GERMAN GOVERNMENT THROUGH THE INTERNATIONAL RED CROSS STATES YOUR HUSBAND SECOND LIEUTENANT CONRAD J. NETTING WHO WAS PREVIOUSLY REPORTED MISSING IN ACTION WAS KILLED IN ACTION TEN JUNE IN EUROPEAN AREA THE SECRETARY OF WAR EXTENDS HIS DEEP SYMPATHY CONFIRMING LETTER FOLLOWS
= DUNLOP ACTING THE ADJUTANT GENERAL

A week later, Katherine wrote her final journal entry.

Dearest Conrad,

Well, this will probably be the last time I shall ever write those beloved words – Dearest Conrad – except perhaps to your son. Yes, I went to Corpus Christi on the 7th and the next day Frances had word to call Charlotte. When she came out of the drug store, I could see she was upset. I immediately thought her father was worse. I was driving and I didn't say anything for a block or two. Then I asked if she wanted to stop for some bread. Then she sort of dropped her head and I reached over and patted her shoulder. She said, "but it's not about me." And I knew at once what it was.

I drove on for a block or two – shocked and stunned and overcome – then I had a desire to be home with your son. I turned a corner and pulled over to the side and just caved in for a moment. It wasn't too long, darling, for uppermost in my mind was – and always will be – Conrad can see me now and I must make him proud of me. Frances suggested I wait and talk to Tennille and so I stayed on and came home with them Saturday.

I feel so strange. I believe all the anguish – wild anguish – was spent when I first knew you were missing and might never return. Now, I feel sad – empty – immeasurably lonely – and sick at the waste of so marvelous a life, the waste of both our lives together. I know you are dead. First – the wire – then the letter – now, a condolence card from General [George C.] Marshall, Chief of Staff – each throws another spadefull on your grave. But above all, I am resigned. I haven't "cried" it out. I've shed tears, but not in abundance. And, although it is not what I prayed, planned, dreamed, hoped for, I am making plans for my life – our lives without you. Our son, of whom you dreamed but never knew about, will live in peace because of your sacrifice and the sacrifice of thousands like you.

I feel no more . . . bitterness as I did when I received that grim wire, ". . . missing in action. . . ." Instead, I feel a resigned peace, for no longer do I have the hopeful prayer of a calm, contented life with you.

I must now fill the place you have partially left with our son. I have begun my plans for a life of work that will give him all you would have given him materially. I have also begun to think of how I can tell him of your great character. Our boy must know you, through me. The words of your citation, "courage, skill, and coolness," will mean much to him [as will] the words of General Marshall that "our people shall not forget what you did." But more than that, he must know the small things: your love for children, your gentleness, your consideration for all. He must know you first as a kind, godly man, second as a hero/warrior.

I have learned many lessons from this great sorrow. I have learned humbleness. I have learned that much as I petition God, He knows what is best. I have learned the futility of bitterness, the strengthening from faith and prayer. I have learned the worth of my memories. And I pray that our peace-loving God will lead our country, our people to an everlasting peace, so that the loss to mankind through your death and all the others will not be made a mockery. I pray God will let peace reign forever as a tribute to your valor. I pray the free people of this land, this world, will never forget nor in any way besmirch the memory of your death.

I have talked to Charlotte regarding a ½ day job in her adv. agency. I will go to work as soon as she will take me on. I won't make much, but it will be something. But above all, I will be laying a firm foundation for a career. I could return to the govt but I want to take from my work more than money alone. I want security, a sense of accomplishment, a future, an interesting job, a pleasant one. As I learn, I can build something on my own hard work and I will. For I want Conrad to be proud of me and through me, of you. I also want him to have everything I can buy for him. I want to fill your shoes as I know you would have, if God had heard and answered my prayer that if one of us had to die, it would be me.

So I shall work hard and long for our son, and I'll make him proud of all he has received from you. Before too *long, I hope to put aside all your insurance and my pension and I will. On Tennille's advice, I will invest all the lump sum I receive over a $1,000 back in war bonds. I am going to write concerning that Socony Vacuum Policy, also. You left your family extremely well provided considering you were only 26 years and 3 days old.*

I intend to see [Rev.] Sam [Capers] in a week about a memorial service. Also, I will give something to the church in memory of the finest husband a girl ever had.

I intend to see about insurance on my own life for Conrad.

Darling, you know, I'm sure, how deeply I love you. I say love because I still do. I haven't stopped and I won't. Always, I love you as much as I did July 17, 1943, and all the days before and all the days since. I just can't stop. But, can you know the need I feel to marry again? When I look forward to emptiness after such happiness, I can't bear it. I hope God will let me be happy, not wildly, consumingly happy as I was with you, for I know I was amongst the chosen for having had you for a while. But quietly happy, the physical side is not so important, tho I will miss you so much – your hands, your kiss, your body. It is having no one interested in my life to the least detail that I miss tremendously. I want companionship – I don't want to live out my life – God knows, how beastly long I shall live – all alone for I'm afraid lest I be twisted, abnormally interested in Conrad or my work. I want a normal life, with a husband who knows my life was you.

I believe if I ever should remarry, it will be long from now and to some older man who, too, has already known the greatest love. For me to marry a young boy – say Bob or Carl or anyone of that type – would be selfish. I believe all men are entitled to having a love such as I gave you. And I cannot give such love twice.

Well, my darling, from October 17, 1942 to June 10, 1944 or to January 8, 1945, really is a terrible, pathetically short time. Yet the love you gave me, the happiness, the joy, the magnificent son – could be copied in no one in a full lifetime. My dear, I am saying goodbye to you now

– until we meet again. Please help me through the hard years to come, help me to do my best for your son and mine, help me keep alive your spirit by never being bitter. I need your help so – you may be dead to others, but you will live forever in my heart. I hate to stop writing for this is my last letter to you. O, my darling, how I love you."

Forever,

Your ~~wife~~ widow

Blurred ink in dime-sized circles throughout this entry must be from tears falling to the pages.

Sometime in February 1945, though Katherine had seemingly processed her grief and ended her writing, she wrote down her thoughts about the day she received the first telegram.

No hell could be as terrible as the one I've lived in since that day last June – only eight months ago – eight months! It seems like eight decades. . . . When I woke, the mockingbird that sat in the lilac tree had already begun his morning's tirade [that would last] from early morning until the late June evening closed with its fireflies and the noises of all the summer insects.

As I lay in a half dream, I thought unwillingly of all the girls I knew who had heard that their husbands were missing or killed. As I counted them over it seemed that all the misfortune of war was falling on my set – my young set. I wondered "What if you get a wire, too. What will you do?" This wasn't the first time, and I had gone over it so often but never with a sense of what it would really be. I didn't know what it would be. I couldn't comprehend what my life would become without him. I visualized myself bravely facing a bitter world – gaunt face, trembling hands, pale eyes. Then, harshly, I dared think that perhaps I would lose his child [and that] burdened me so.

The thought was too real, and with the blind confidence of youth I shook off this morbid vivisection and began to plan the day. I would finish painting the lawn chairs, I would bake a cake – a chocolate one to greet my mother . . . I would wash my hair. O, I was so full of plans, but first I would write my daily letter to him – write

how beastly long I shall live – all alone
for I'm afraid lest I be twisted –
abnormally interested in Conrad
or my work – I want a normal
life – with a husband who knows
my life was you – I believe if
I ever should re-marry, it will
be long from now and to some
older man who, too, has already
known the greatest love – to me
to marry a young boy – a sob-
on Coul or anyone of that type –
would be selfish – I believe all
men are entitled to having a
love such as I gave you – And
I could give such love twice –

with my darling – from October 14, 1942 to June 10, 1944
to January 8, 1945, really, is a
terribly, pathetically short time –
but the love you gave me – the
happiness, the joy – the magnificent son – could be copied
by no one in a full life time.
My dear – I am saying goodbye
to you now – until we meet
again – Please help me through
the hard years to come – Help
me to do my best for your son
and mine – help me keep alive
your spirit by never being bitter.
I need your help so – you may be
dead to others – but you will

A tear-stained page in a diary was among the mementos
discovered in a forgotten footlocker in 1994.

it in the morning when sun and people and work ahead
would keep some of the lonesomeness from creeping in to
trouble him long after I had forgotten the words. I started
this soon after he left. We had so many nights to remember
poignantly, but the mornings were – just mornings, the
time for him to hurry off to the field at dawn.

In that last delicious moment before I stirred to arise,
before the sun began to stifle and sear, I heard the steps on
the porch – slow, meditated steps. I was fascinated – and
then, a swift glance at the clock, strangely afraid and cold.
I was cold on a June morning in Texas! It was too early for
any special delivery mail, which never came before nine.
Too early for a peddler or salesman or visitor or delivery
boy. As my mind searched for some explanation, I heard
his faint, foretelling knock.

I pulled my bunglesome body up and covered the
swollen shape of my body with an old seersucker wrapper
of my mother's. I opened the door, blindly signed the
proffered form, tore open the wire and searched for one
word – would it be "wounded," O God, please, let him be
wounded, not killed.

Katherine's mercurial feelings could make a compelling study. Early in her journal she writes, "in the future," followed within days by "if you are dead." She changes course again, saying, "I shall never accept [your death]. Take care of yourself, and hurry home." Soon enough she changes again, writing, "If you are dead" and "too bad you are gone." Another reversal, "Come home to me," followed by "he died in a glorious way." Her volatile emotions continue until she ends her journal, when she says she is, at last, resigned to Conrad's death. Her last entry repeats an earlier admission: "I know you are dead." And she closes looking to the future: "I am making plans."

This introspective writing was far less common in the 1940s than today. Katherine's gift for words and the quiet confidence journaling gave her probably helped her heal. Her communication, though one-sided, may be what kept her steady through her turmoil.

In February 1945, a month after her last journal entry, Katherine wrote to a friend: "I've tried to take it well, but I'm a sissy. Gosh, when I think I'll never see him again as long as I live I nearly perish. And poor little Con has lost so much. Sons need their fathers so. I wish I could have died instead of Conrad. I'll never know a more wonderful person if I live to be a thousand. It seems such a pity that so fine a man should die when the world needs him so. But that is that and I just have to take it for the simple reason that it is all I can do."

My great-grandfather, Conrad Sr., wrote to me for my third birthday: "I turn with deep affection and love thanking daily our Heavenly Father for you. May He guide and protect you in the years to come so that you grow up in the likeness of your Daddie, who was my pal."

Family archives do not reveal if my grandmother ever replaced the service flag in her window, this one with a gold star to represent a family member killed in action.

✳ ✳ ✳

Once my father's death was official, my mother had to begin processing her beloved's personal effects through a cumbersome bureaucratic system. As devastating as that was, where was his body? Was there a body? The Army had no answers to these questions then, and wouldn't for months more.

In early 1945, about nine months after the crash, my mother still had no body to mourn, no ritual to manage, and no gravesite to bring her grief to a close. Such rites would have helped make the transition from wife to widow. Not yet twenty-two years old, she might not have had much experience at such rites, but her instincts must have been screaming for some end to the torment.

Conrad John Netting IV, held by his mother, receives his late father's Air Medal during a ceremony at Brooks Field in San Antonio in February 1945.

By April, the footlocker arrived. In it were the 150 or so letters she wrote to him from the time she left Florida until he died. We don't know when, but eventually she carefully folded each article of clothing, arranged the magazines, pictures, and flight log, placed his letters in small stacks and tied them with a narrow ribbon, and finally did the same with her letters. She added a box or more of mothballs and sealed the footlocker with all these pieces inside. This is what Emily Dickinson called "sweeping up the heart, the solemnest of industries enacted upon earth." Maybe my mother put the footlocker in the garage, out of view, and returned to her room in the house. Other than the absence of friends and family, was this much different from a funeral?

Months later, Bob Netting passed on an unofficial report he had uncovered indicating that my father's grave had been discovered. My mother wrote to the Adjutant General on November 13, 1945, asking for confirmation that the grave existed. The Quartermaster General responded on December 7. "The official German burial report, received in this office through captured enemy records, indicates that the remains of your husband were interred in Saint-Michel-des-Andaines, France. When this reported burial has been verified by the American Graves Registration Service, and your husband's remains have been removed to an established American Cemetery, you will be advised."

Other documents I discovered confirmed that the government knew on March 17, 1945, that my father's grave had been located and confirmed. Why the Army didn't relay this comforting news to my mother and instead waited for her to write to them eight months later is inexplicable.

In a letter dated on her birthday, March 11, 1946, she learned from a brigadier general that my dad was buried with other Allies in a temporary cemetery near Gorron, a small Norman town in France. In October 1947, the Army asked what she wished to do with my dad's remains. She elected to leave them in France at a new American cemetery. Finally, on April 18, 1949, almost five years after his death, the Army wrote that my dad's remains were permanently interred "side-by-side with comrades who also gave their lives for their country. Customary military services were conducted over the grave at the time of burial. You may rest assured that this final interment was conducted with fitting dignity and solemnity and that the gravesite will be carefully and conscientiously maintained in perpetuity by the United States Government."

Almost one-fourth of the dead in World War II, 93,242, are buried overseas. Should my mother have brought his body home? By then she had a nearly five-year-old son and a career and was dating aimlessly. She could have reopened her grief, gathered the relatives (Conrad's grandparents, however, had died together in an automobile crash in 1947), reserved the church, and called the funeral home. Or she could be resigned that her mourning had ended when she sealed the foot-locker. The disadvantage was that there would be no nearby grave for us to visit. She solved this by installing in the Netting family cemetery plot in San Antonio a duplicate of the cross that would mark Conrad's grave in France.

* * *

My father didn't live to enjoy the astonishing success of his 4th Fighter Group. After the war, the Army recognized it as having the highest number of German planes destroyed, 1,016. The 4th was the first group to fly into German airspace (July 28, 1943) and the first to engage enemy aircraft over Paris and Berlin. Eventually, the War Department awarded the 4th Fighter Group the Distinguished Unit Citation, its highest unit honor. This success had its price, and Conrad helped pay it. The Eighth Air Force had nearly 47,000 casualties and, of those, 26,000 fatalities; 6,656 aircraft never returned. The Eighth incurred half of all Air Corps casualties in all theatres of World War II. Of the sixteen pilots in Conrad's training squadron in Florida, 69 percent would be lost in action, most during their first six weeks of combat; five, almost one-third, would be killed.

* * *

Over the years, my mother made occasional attempts at keeping a diary. Though sporadic, the entries were honest and revealing. One came from the winter of 1955, possibly provoked by a lumpectomy she had. She wrote:

> [The Nettings Jr.] are being exceedingly friendly and
> I am grateful for their many kindnesses. Still, I have a

dreadful reaction to being with them because for hours
thereafter I am so terribly lonely for their son. God alone
knows the emptiness in my heart and my inability to join
the more normal people who can – or appear to – keep the
past under control. There is no way for me to forget.

I know how wrong I am, but I can never forget
promising that sweet man that I would love him and him
alone always. "Can he be betrayed?" I argue, not because
there is or ever has been one I would love, but only because
I have been led to believe such an attitude is not healthy.
Healthy or not, he is my love and I am thrilled by the
thought that I will be with him again. I know it! Jesus
promised and if I, with all my weaknesses and mortal sin,
can keep this promise made so long ago, how can I think
Jesus will let me down?

I love life tremendously and tremble at cancer, yet
paradoxically I resent the long empty years 'till I am with
Conrad again. I find myself whispering his name in the
night and the tears are there for him. Tears do not lessen
the well of grief, but for a time they seem to wash the pain
away. The emotions are numbed and sleep comes quickly.

The results of the biopsy were negative.

Later, during the same period, she wrote about finding a few letters she and Conrad had written each other. "I am a human pack rat and feel utterly disloyal and unfaithful if I destroy the thoughts of one I care about. Naturally, I read a letter or two [between Conrad and me] and though it hurts, I am reminded of the most magnificent life I had with him. That he would want me will always amaze and thrill me. So honest, so good, so decent – never lived a more perfect man. And I would not change one second of my life if it meant losing an instant of having loved and been loved by him. A small price to pay for my two Conrads is to spend the remaining years remembering one, mothering the other, and loving both so deeply."

On her fortieth birthday in 1963 she wrote a letter to herself, a diary update:

My forty years have been eventful. Superficially, they
have been crowded with my friends and my work. [But]

the foundation has been my ever-constant family. My son has been more than I could hope or pray for. The center of my life is my husband. Though he has been dead almost nineteen years, he still shapes my life. I have earnestly tried to fall in love again and again. There have been many infatuations, but no true love.

It is a lonely thing, and it would be too bitter to bear if God had not been so generous in all the gifts I have. Everything, I seem to have in abundance. Perhaps as a compensation for the loss of the life Conrad and I might have had. My wonderful son, my family, my work, my friends, my church – in all these, I find success and fulfillment. I hope [the future] brings one thing – love.

At the University of Texas at Austin in the mid-1960s, I enrolled in the Army R.O.T.C. program, intending to be commissioned as a second lieutenant on graduation. At the height of the Vietnam War, this seemed prudent, though it must have petrified my mother to know that I might fight in that war. In my senior year, I learned that because I was the "sole surviving son of a deceased veteran," I was not obliged to serve in the military. I, therefore, could quit the R.O.T.C. program, relinquish my many R.O.T.C. credit hours, and be honorably dismissed from the program.

As I struggled with that decision, my mother wrote me, "When it came time for your father to enlist (as you know, he was not required to serve in the war because his work as a petroleum engineer was essential, and he elected to join the Air Corps even though he was not required to serve), the Air Corps was delighted to have him. When he died, they couldn't send enough lovely memos, medals, condolences, legal aid officers – but as soon as the dust dies down, it is a different story. It isn't easy to have lost your husband and two or three children you expected to have and a life you expected to have." Based on practicality and patriotism, I decided to accept my R.O.T.C. commission, serving two years as a quartermaster officer. Because of my "sole surviving son" status, I was exempt from service in Vietnam.

My mother also wrote: "It was your arrival that caused me to become active in the church. When your father and I married, I needed the church very much. I was frightened. Then, when you arrived, I needed it even more . . . I would trade all we have to have your father back."

As she coped with an empty nest at forty-nine, she wrote to me after she saw a movie that affected her deeply. "Your father looked to me to help him become the independent man he wanted to be. Indeed, he was already this independent man, as strong and individual as you are today, but he needed more time to recognize this."

My mother would heal, though never entirely. Using her inherent intelligence and without benefit of a college degree, she worked hard and helped develop an extremely successful drug company. She worked for it in San Antonio for thirty-one years, helping to sell it to a far larger company along the way. Not content with early retirement, at fifty-six she opened a management consulting business and, along with running that business, was executive director of a large San Antonio charity. She remarried in 1972 and remained devoted to her second husband until her death in 1993 after a long, debilitating illness.

And so, from our earthly perspective, my mother lived without her first love for almost fifty years. But maybe the bible she so steadfastly studied comforted her: "A little while and you shall not see me and, again a little while and you shall see me." Soon enough, she saw him again.

PART TWO

INTRODUCTION TO PART TWO

Coincidences are God's way of remaining anonymous.
—*Doris Lessing*

Neither Pauleen nor I remember what we were doing that Saturday morning in February 2002. By noon we drifted to the kitchen, had a lunch that is forgotten, and heard the mail arrive. We ignored it for a few minutes while we finished the dishes, and then I began looking at the unrequested catalogs, credit card offers, and monthly bills.

A large envelope loomed at the bottom of the stack, with peculiar markings on its face, showing a return address of Paris. As I opened the bulky envelope addressed to me, I tried to process why I would get anything from France. A scam? A chain letter? What bizarre scheme was behind this?

I pulled out the contents and began to read the topmost letter, hand printed on European-sized paper. I was stunned as I began to realize that, for a second dramatic time, my father's legacy as I perceived it was about to change.

------------ ★ ------------

CHAPTER TEN

Louis Grandin of
Saint-Michel-des-Andaines

He was forty-seven years old and restless. His life wasn't his own anymore, and for the second time. This time, at least, he was at home and surrounded by friends he had grown up with. But they too were leading unsettled lives. Discontent and hopelessness seemed everywhere, not only in his village, Saint-Michel-des-Andaines, but, he had heard, in the whole of his beloved Norman province. The occupiers, the dictators, the conquerors – the Germans! They were the cause of it all.

In 1940, 500,000 of them (one for every eighty Frenchmen) had goose-stepped into France, occupying the northern half, that part closest to their next target, England. All along the English Channel they were building fortifications, using every available Gallic workman (some 250,000) and every ounce of French cement (800,000 tons monthly). The conceit of it all: constructing defenses with French labor and materials that would ensure the Normans' continued subjugation. Though the coastline was eighty kilometers away, the German military truck convoys rumbled through his village.

By early summer 1944, after four years of occupation, Normandy was enduring endless hardships. The 200,000 German troops were fed Normandy's milk and meat. The locals wore clothes that had already lasted four years and were looking tattered. Cars were rarely in evidence, replaced by bicycles. The black market was thriving. Debilitating diseases were more evident. And, as a further misery, a drought that year had kept the farmers' production below normal levels.

Louis Grandin had seen it all before. In 1914, during the Great War, an earlier generation of Germans captured him and held him prisoner for three years. He was reduced to a mild form of slavery, kowtowing to every German demand. Being efficient – you had to give them that – the Germans learned he was a joiner, a skilled carpenter.

Even though he had only been at his trade for a few years, he was accomplished at making furniture, doors, windows, moulding, and other complicated woodwork. His plans had always been to make fine wood products for his friends and the villagers, not for his enemy. Yet he was a prisoner in Germany, doing just that. What could he do to even the score? Nothing – then.

Over twenty years later, the same story was unfolding. Married now, he and Marie-Louise and their five children had established themselves as essential members of their agrarian community. His genial neighbors had come to respect his skills and judgment. Almost everyone in Saint-Michel-des-Andaines needed those skills at one time or another, certainly on their deaths, for he made their coffins. He was an entrepreneur, both in the English sense of the word, as a businessman, and in the Old French meaning – an undertaker.

Marie-Louise, ten years younger than Louis, also had a mind for business. Noticing that their town of Saint-Michel-des-Andaines needed basic supplies, she opened a convenience store, to use today's term, in a space adjacent to her home. She lived in the center of town not more than six blocks from anyone. This central location would save her customers the four-kilometer walk into the larger La Ferté-Macé. Though that walk was pleasant enough and went by the town cemetery, which could trigger memories of friends and family who had died, the short stroll to Marie-Louise's was better. Further, gossipy news could be exchanged. The store was across from the town hall, and so a customer could expect to see the mayor or deputy mayor and from time to time offer a voter's opinion.

Also adjacent to the Grandin home was Louis's workshop. And sidewalks, just as important here as in other parts of the world, con-nected that home to the school a few steps away. The Grandins and their neighbors were close-knit. With two sources of income in the family, they had all they needed and much of what they wanted.

As would befit a joiner, everything in Louis's life since his release from Germany was a good fit, a tight fit. He could see how his life would play out; he was a respected player in a village largely unchanged over the centuries. But when the Germans insinuated themselves into this strategic part of Normandy, all expectations changed. They had come to frustrate him once again.

The first frustration was the German officer who usurped the upstairs bedroom. This meant Marie-Louise would clean up after him, both in the bedroom and in the bath. Linens and supplies were her responsibility, and no doubt he required her to furnish them without payment. No doubt, too, family life revolved around his schedule.

The next frustration was that the Grandins had to feed the Germans in the family's dining room. After all, Teutonic efficiency dictated that one's meals be in the same location as one's sleeping quarters. The German soldiers would, unannounced, want certain food, and Marie-Louise would cook it. She could be shot if she refused. One time they wanted rabbit. She said she had no rabbit. They insisted on her pet rabbits. If she didn't kill them, they would. So she killed them, and cooked and served them to her occupiers. She was afraid.

The most satisfying way of retaliating against the German demands was developed in Luxembourg. When Luxembourgers knew they could not mount a military defense against the German invasion in May 1940, they strung barbed wire across roads, closed bridges, and generally upset German plans. They called this passive defense, but the French called it *La Résistance* – the resistance – and the rest of the world would call it the same. The resistance in Normandy was intense, with more than 1,000 attacks launched on June 5–6 alone. Organized resistance was not active in Saint-Michel-des-Andaines, however, and confrontations were rare; the villagers were circumspect around the Germans, who were throughout the town on foot and in convoys. Louis was again a captive of the occupiers, though not technically their prisoner. He must have seethed at the false German authority and harassment that he, and especially Marie-Louise, suffered. If no organized resistance existed, what were his options? His animosity toward the Germans, suppressed since World War I, was intense.

Louis did not have the expected look of a carpenter. He had evolved into a dead ringer for Santa Claus, minus the red suit and beard. He was hearty and jolly, and he wore rimless glasses. Louis was, of course, a product of his environment, so his pear shape and rosy cheeks might be the result of Normandy's calvados liqueur, Camembert cheese, and crusty bread. Stylish he was not, but he was a perfect fit in Saint-

Michel-des-Andaines. His children knew that his Santa Claus look was deceptive, for he could administer fatherly justice swiftly with whatever two-by-four happened to be at hand. He was serious on the surface but jovial and loving underneath.

In this part of Normandy there were villages every five or ten kilometers; some had grown into towns while others seemed unchanged. In every village, small houses hugged the roadways and displayed dazzling flowers in every color, many seemingly untended. The buildings, cars, and people complemented each other as if in a tableaux. Outside the villages were the extraordinary hedgerows, called *bocage*, or "box country" by the French, which were originally fence lines that defined fields and ownership. They were developed by Celtic farmers before the Roman era and over the centuries became impenetrable with untamed growth. If good fences make for good neighbors, then these hedgerows would produce eternal harmony.

As a successful joiner, Louis Grandin had created a lifestyle around harmony, balance, and interlocking parts. A mismatched element would make the whole product unworthy. Everything he did, and everything he wanted his family to do, centered on the right fit. And now it was denied him. What options did he have?

Louis Grandin, the French carpenter who secretly made Lieutenant Netting's coffin, in the 1950s.

★

CHAPTER ELEVEN

A Fateful Strafing Run Over Normandy, II

The occupied French could never relax amid the steady drone of trucks heading toward the coast, the Luftwaffe on patrol protecting the German investment in men and machines below, and the Germans living in the Norman towns. The residents of La Ferté-Macé and Saint-Michel-des-Andaines had steeled themselves to these encroachments in their lives and could tell instantly when something changed the set order. They watched with practiced eyes for some unusual event, some break in a pattern that might have negative implications for them and their families. No one in the area had been killed from any war cause in the four years of occupation, and no one wanted to be the first. They were careful to be nondescript in their demeanor and speech so that the Germans would have no reason to single them out.

The children, too, were guarded in all they did; they knew that a wrong word, a single misstep could result in serious trouble. This June, with school out, they saw each other in the streets and at the few meager playgrounds. Many worked alongside their parents, especially those with unending farm chores. The men in uniform, the roar of the trucks, and the occasional tank through town were hardly worth a look. Still, they knew to be invisible and not draw the Germans' attention.

Eleven-year-old Michel Grandin, eldest child of Louis and Marie-Louise, was wiry, almost skeletal, with a pointed jaw. He bore hardly any resemblance to his father. From the time he was six until now, more than half of his conscious life, he had lived under German occupation. He had watched his parents suffer the burden of the occupied. He was grateful that none of them had suffered physically.

Michel had deep-set eyes the blue of a summer sky. They could quickly absorb a scene. His eyes could also be welcoming, making a friend before words were spoken. They could seek approval, registering an openness and vulnerability he could have never verbally expressed. But more than that, his eyes seemed to have a ready supply of tears.

Despite the German presence, Michel and his friends could get into mischief. So Louis kept his two-by-four board handy.

That summer, the children of Michel's village had no inkling of the historic events that were unfolding. Had they been able to float down the nearby River Orne toward the English Channel, they would have passed Caen and seen German planes landing. As the river met the channel, they would have seen German soldiers swimming and relaxing in the refreshing channel water. Had they been able to float a mile out to sea, they would have seen the British submarines positioned as navigational aides for the fleet that would soon arrive. But without the benefit of hindsight they could not be expected to observe anything more than the routine of that Norman weekend.

Beginning on June 6, 1944, everyone could tell that the routine had changed. No longer were the Luftwaffe cruising the skies. A different plane dominated. Activity was furious. The Germans were crazier than ever. Some said that the invasion had started, but without radios no one could be sure. No one heard officially what had happened. But they could sense it. The long-anticipated invasion had begun.

Four days later, the Normans felt that maybe their occupiers would lose, that the Allies could invade and win. How long would it take? When would they know? They were terrified; the battlefield was at their doorsteps.

Along the road to La Ferté-Macé was the Saint-Michel-des-Andaines cemetery. Its stone cross, weathered but straight, at least thirty feet tall, was like a Christian beacon with an almost magnetic pull. The low stone wall surrounding the revered quarter-acre protected the scores of graves inside. Their markers were solid, spare, and cold. The gravel paths between each family's plot, unbroken by plants or greenery, added to the Spartan feeling. The villagers who visited, and there were many, did not think of these things but rather of their ancestors and of paying homage to them. Even a brief visit seemed to revive visitors' spirits as they reflected on their personal histories.

Finding quiet in the roadside graveyard was not easy. "A munitions supply dump was not far from Saint-Michel-des-Andaines but on another road," Michel remembered. The most practical route to the beachhead from the dump took the military trucks by the cemetery. The rumbling of full trucks heading to the front and empty ones returning to the dump, passing each other like ants on a march, interrupted meditation within the walls. The German sentries stationed at the cemetery didn't contribute to one's peace of mind.

Then came the day that the people of Saint-Michel-des-Andaines would remember for the rest of their lives. "That morning, the sky was cloudless above Saint-Michel-des-Andaines, a city still occupied by the enemy," Michel Grandin said later. It was Saturday, a day for chores, or a visit at the Grandins' store, or a walk to La Ferté-Macé, taking care to avoid the German trucks. After breakfast, Michel was playing outside.

Not a kilometer away, off the road to La Ferté-Macé and behind the cemetery, Françis Toutain, a friend of Michel's, was tending to his chores in the weathered outbuildings of his family's farm. His chickens were an important part of the farm's production, providing eggs in a time when eggs were treasured commodities. The enemy trucks roared past on the main road just 300 meters from the chickens, keeping them agitated.

About 10 a.m., Michel heard the noise: "A German tank truck appeared on the road going from La Ferté-Macé to Saint-Michel-des-Andaines. It was followed by a second one, then a third and a fourth. The trucks were full of fuel. We heard the firing. All of a sudden the trucks were burning. Nobody from the trucks was firing at the planes. The German soldiers by the road were firing at the planes. At the same time, we heard a noise in the air. Several fighters, flying in formation, appeared suddenly above La Forêt d'Andaine [the Andaine Forest]. We heard the rattling of machine guns and our parents ordered us to come back into the house and stay inside."

The trucks were making their way toward Saint-Michel-des-Andaines. The U.S. Army's report recounted: "Pilot of subject aircraft was strafing a German truck along a small country road leading to village of Saint-Michel-des-Andaines. Prior to the truck blowing up, driver vaulted hedge into ditch, and pilot, attempting to kill him, banked to the left."

The wingman, to the pilot's left and rear, in his slipstream, recalled: "He just turned and went right in. . . . And I was coming right behind him. I had to stop firing. I couldn't fire until he pulled away. But as soon as he pulled away, I started firing, and I could see [his face]. I was right next to [his plane]."

The leader of Becky Blue section, Lt. Donald Emerson, who was flying with Lt. Conrad J. Netting III the day he claimed a Me 410 destroyed, wrote in his report a few days later: "[The pilot] said he was going in first and I watched him make a very tight turning pass to port firing while in a sharp bank. When he started to pull up he was still turning to port and I saw him pull streamers [resulting from extreme pressure to pull up]."

At that instant Françis Toutain saw the leading fighter plane veer out of control just above his home and the satellite farm buildings. The plane passed not twenty-five meters overhead. The section leader reported: "Not realizing the close proximity of bordering trees, [the plane] crashed between two large oaks. At that moment his plane seemed to flick to the left and he went into the woods on his back. The aircraft exploded." Françis ran to the house. Later, his neighbors would report: "[The pilot] must be a hero because he avoided the farmhouse. He did not fall on the farm, but just beyond it. Only one chicken was killed."

Michel said, "I heard the big noise and went outside. We saw the smoke." That was all he would later remember. "But after the noise my father said we were going to stay inside of the house. Later, my father was told that an Allied plane had just crashed not far from the cemetery. The pilot had not survived. My father went to the crash site but forbade me to go, because the ammunition was near the burning kerosene."

The American report continued: "The aircraft exploded on contact, the pilot being thrown clear . . . He was dead on being reached by the French forestry guard. Germans were on the scene immediately, and confiscated all the pilot papers except his AGO card [Adjutant General's Order, used for identification], which was turned over to the mayor of the village who subsequently turned it over to the French gendarmerie in Marseilles."

In the official German report: "One Mustang crashed about three hundred meters left side of street La Ferté-Macé to St.-Michel-des-Andaines. Aircraft was apparently downed by infantry weapons of station Field Fest." This was not the case, however, as reported by three other sources. The Saint-Michel-des-Andaines archives report that the crash was caused by a sudden lack of speed. Michel Grandin recalled that the Germans did not hit the plane. And the section leader, who was killed later that year on Christmas Day, wrote, "I do not think this accident was due to enemy action."

The local newspaper later reported: "A park ranger saw the plane go down. He alerted the parish priest, Abbé Eugène Hochet, and Louis Grandin, the village carpenter. But the German military command was already at the scene." The German report said that English and American money was found on the body along with personal papers including dog tags, passport, personal cards, and one picture. No doubt who was in that picture.

Michel Grandin said, "[My father] saw the name 'Conrad J' . . . on the plane part, which he got from the forest ranger." And the local newspaper reported much later: "The carpenter had picked up a piece of the plane's cabin. On it the pilot had painted, 'Conrad J.' In any case, there was not enough information to identify the pilot."

Identified or not, what did villagers think when they saw the Teutonic name "Conrad"? Any number of clues would have proved the pilot was an ally: the plane, probably still showing its U.S. markings, the strafing run against a German convoy, and the actions of the Germans at the scene. To the credit of the French, they were ready to treat the noble pilot to the burial any human should have.

An American report, written six months later, said, "All salvageable units of the aircraft were taken by the Germans for technical examination." Michel Grandin recalled, however: "The Germans were not interested in the site. They were busy doing other things. The Germans made a report of the crash so they would have statistics correct." Other reports say the Americans salvaged the plane parts; still others say the French took them into storage. The only thing that is certain is that the plane's largest parts were gone.

———————— ★ ————————

CHAPTER TWELVE

A Forbidden Burial

Saint-Michel-des-Andaines was galvanized. A war death, incurred for their freedom, was at their threshold. No longer were the battles distant. The aroma of burning kerosene was malodorous and undeniable. The townspeople must have felt a terrible hollowness. Powerless to openly fight for their own freedom, bypassed by the French resistance, and marginalized by the Germans, how would they respond? A human body lay disfigured in the underbrush not a stone's throw from town. To leave it there was un-Christian and unacceptable.

Michel had every signal that this day would be momentous. At midmorning the brrrp-brrrp of machine guns cut through the quiet countryside. Then the terrible noise of the crash like a thunderclap. Then a mushroom cloud, black as pitch, plumed from the explosion. Michel wanted to run to the site, just a kilometer from his house. But his father said to wait. And his father was to be obeyed. After the Germans had completed their inspection of the crash site, Louis went to it and found the pilot still strapped in the plane. Cautiously, he lifted the body from the cockpit and laid it beside the plane, contrary to the American pilot's report.

Later, at Louis's home, the priest and the ranger came. In muffled voices, the three men discussed the options. Agreement was quick. Michel remembered, "The forest ranger came to my father first thing in the afternoon and asked him to make a casket. That was routine when a death occurred in the village, because he was the only carpenter."

While officially not an undertaker, Louis had extensive experience with the customs of funerals. No matter that a funeral for an American under the Germans' noses would be difficult. To conduct a funeral in this time of war would bring order for a moment and the remembrance of a more civilized life.

In his father's workshop, Michel was comforted by the familiar smell of fresh wood, oils, and metal. The cramped room gave little idea of the sun outside. Michel wondered why all the windows were closed. Was it because of the crash that morning?

Louis began his work with the tools he had used throughout his career. He worked at the pitted workbench that gave evidence of the miss hits of the hammer and the holes from errant nails. Michel watched as his father formed a rough six-foot box. He had seen such boxes before. After an hour or so, progress was noticeable. Louis Grandin would need six more hours to make the coffin; the funeral could be held that evening.

Unexpectedly, there was a quick rap at the door. The dreaded Germans entered. Sharp words were exchanged, and Louis stopped his work. The Germans had never seemed so agitated as in the last four days. And now this. Something was happening. The strafing, the crash, the fireball, the coffin. This day he would remember.

How did Louis feel working on the coffin? Would this be an outlet for his frustration, which began in World War I?

"My father was a joiner and his workshop was then under the Germans' control," Michel remembered. "Without the guards' knowledge he set to work and started making a coffin so that he and the parish priest could bury [the pilot] with dignity." The official record reports, "Our joiner, a veteran of World War I, did not hesitate to perform this task, despite the menacing presence of two German sentries standing in front of his workshop." Soon the Germans pieced together that the village was about to honor their enemy, and they forbade it. Entreaties that this was a Christian soldier and deserved respect went unheeded. They commanded Louis Grandin to stop his work. Later he took his tools to the school and finished the coffin there.

In the classroom, as dust motes, noticeable through the late evening sun, floated around him, Louis went to work. Michel said: "I remember seeing my father make the casket. My father did that for [the pilot] because it was his duty, what he had to do. He couldn't bury him any other way, though he could have been severely punished if they had heard him. My father took care of the pilot." "Took care of" were Michel's words to convey that his father acted as undertaker and all that implies.

At dusk, almost 10 p.m. that time of year, the ranger and farmer slipped through the back entrance of the school. The joiner showed them the coffin. Its simple lines were similar to those he had made dozens of times, but its contents would be exceptional. They balanced it on their shoulders and walked to the still smoldering wreckage, out of sight of their occupiers. They were not resistance fighters – not many in the area were – and sneaking about against German orders was foreign to them. Once clear of the sentries on the road, they stayed by the hedgerows, past the farm buildings, across the ravine, and into the forest. The smell of spent kerosene filled the air. A few meters farther on, they saw the village priest, positioned by the burnt wreckage. Stepping across blackened trees downed by the hurtling plane, they saw the body, barely recognizable as such.

"My father," Michel recalled, "took care of the body." Michel is again saying what is usually indelicate to speak of. "Nobody was supposed to go. Only Germans. He went with three or four others, taking the casket with him. At the site, they put the body in the casket." Abbé Hochet said the prayers and pronounced the blessing, no doubt in French and Latin: "May Thy perpetual light shine upon him. May he and all the souls of the faithful departed rest in peace."

After sprinkling the body with Holy water, they closed the coffin and took it to the Saint-Michel-des-Andaines cemetery, just a short walk away. They buried my father in an unused plot, marking the grave with a wooden cross. Michel said: "My father fixed to it a piece of the aircraft and wrote on it the name of the pilot: Conrad J. The priest coordinated all the procedures: meeting, burial, and benediction. I wanted to go with the priest, to put some Holy water from the church [on the body] but was not allowed to go because I was too young."

The next morning, a Sunday, Louis again told Michel not to go to the site.

Souvenez-vous dans vos prières
de l'âme de

Monsieur l'Abbé Eugène HOCHET
Doyen Honoraire
Curé de Saint-Michel-des-Andaines
(Orne)

Abbé Eugène Hochet, the parish priest in Saint-Michel-des-Andaines, who conducted the forbidden burial ceremony for Lt. Netting.

Later, in rare defiance, he went. The plane was pieces of metal everywhere, and the motor, once a perfect piece of engineering, was mangled in its self-made hole. Michel didn't touch anything and left after an hour.

Normally the townspeople would have gathered for a funeral. Nazi policy allowed no such displays for the enemy. But the Germans couldn't be everywhere, and word spread quickly of the bold steps taken by the few in the forest.

As the predawn darkness slipped away, villagers began to gather in the cemetery to lay bundles of flowers on the grave. Years later Michel said: "People took the flowers to the cemetery but not all at once. A little at a time. The flowers were from their gardens." People came from La Ferté-Macé and Saint-Michel-des-Andaines, on their way to church this Sunday morning. Those for whom Conrad died were coming from all corners to place flowers on his grave.

Flowering a grave is a universal custom, but especially so for the military dead. On the first American Memorial Day in 1868, Gen. John Logan said, "Let us, then, at the time appointed gather around their sacred remains and garland the passionless mounds above them with the choicest flowers of spring-time."

Eventually, there was a mountain of flowers on the grave. Michel wrote later, "When the Germans went past the cemetery and saw this huge pile of flowers, they placed guards at the gate and barred the way to the villagers for several days." Perhaps the Germans feared that a large crowd of Normans could get beyond their control. Still the townspeople paid homage to the pilot. Far from his native country and family, he could rest in peace.

The Allied victory in Normandy was slow and costly. By late July, six weeks after D-Day, Allied holdings extended only ninety kilometers along the coast and ten to twenty kilometers inland. Caen was liberated on July 9, 1944. This glacial pace resulted from trying to cross the endless boxes created by the hedgerows, perhaps thirty such boxes to the mile. But three weeks after that, on August 19, they had taken all of Normandy. On August 25, they rumbled into Paris.

Almost 37,000 Allies died and 210,000 were injured. Two hundred thousand buildings were destroyed. In Vesly, which took the brunt of Patton's thrust, 92 percent of the townspeople lost their homes. Caen, the ancient capital of Normandy and the center of German troop concentration, was rubble, with 60 percent of its buildings in ruins.

The war continued in Europe until May 1945 and in Japan until that August. The demobilization in Europe then gathered steam. Men were heading home. Equipment was left in each country, abandoned for scrap, or purposefully destroyed, including thousands of American aircraft. In 2002, only 275 P-51s existed, with 153 in flying condition.

Samuel Hynes wrote in *The Wall Street Journal:* "The notion of the Good War is a myth, of course. It reduces the war story to a black-and-white parable in which the world's right-minded people defeat the world's evil. It says nothing of the unpleasantness of that war . . . We need to know [the truth], so that we will not allow ourselves to grow nostalgic for the Good War and the greatest generation, but will remember the pain, the waste, the cruelty and the dying."

CHAPTER THIRTEEN

———— ★ ————

Growing Up

Michel Grandin had few carefree days in his youth. First there were the German occupiers, and then, for another year, the liberators were fortifying supply lines and positions for the Allies. By war's end he could have felt robbed of his youth. But that was not Michel's way nor the way of many of his contemporaries.

In their family of five children, Louis and Marie-Louise could expect at least one child to carry on the carpentry trade. Michel was that child. At his father's workbench he began his carpentry career, one that takes time and patience. He no doubt also learned about patriotism and valor. How often did his mind wander back to that day of burning and death? No matter. Nothing could be done now, these many years later.

Michel married Louisette Tete, spending the early part of their wedding night carving for her a three-dimensional scene of a dining-room table and chairs, an act that would later generate guffaws from his children. He affected the look of a Gallic James Dean, complete with T-shirt, sunglasses, motorcycle, and hand-rolled cigarette dangling between two fingers. He passed through that stage, and by 1962 he and Louisette had four children living in Michel's ancestral house.

His warm, welcoming eyes and ready smile masked the emotions just underneath. He was an admirable man, one to be next to, to listen to. As you knew him better, you sensed a rare connectedness. He was relaxed and secure, but he was also vulnerable.

Louisette supported him at every opportunity. Her long, thick hair, deep voice, and ready intelligence were the perfect complement for Michel. When he was quiet, she would talk, as if on his cue. Her home was her realm, unpretentious and white-glove clean. She was proud of it and of her family, and she wasn't shy about taking charge.

With Louis's death in 1960, Michel, then twenty-seven, lost a father, mentor, coach, and historical resource. He must have regretted not learning more from his father. His handkerchief would quickly appear whenever he spoke of Louis, ready for a furtive dab at the eyes. He was a quiet man who spoke only infrequently. Around the more outgoing Louis, he must have absorbed all that Louis said.

What did Louis tell him about that memorable day? Zooming around Normandy on his motorcycle, would he even want to hear the story again? Apparently yes, because over time he felt he had lost a brother in that American plane. Years passed, and Michel took on the daily obligations of family, work, and community. Often he forgot about the childhood filled with occupiers, officials, and orders from both. But the long days in his shop would bring back the unfinished business of Conrad J. and the disquieting feeling that he had not done all he could.

* * *

Much as the Grandin family had done, my family sought balance in the years that followed the calamitous events of June 1944. Once my mother had sealed the footlocker, a ritual that replaced the more formal funeral she couldn't have, she had to move to the reality of raising her child as a single parent, earning a living, and seeking a new direction for her social life. Her biggest uncertainty was raising a son without a father. The war had made many widows the heads of their households, but they were still a minute percentage. Her practical inclinations must have tilted toward a new mate and a stepfather for me. But her heart yearned for Conrad. Finding balance would be her daily test.

I had no lack of male influences after the war. Randall, my father's best friend, was still single and, due to a shortage of housing and personal funds, moved back with his parents, my mother, and me. Another brother, Jimmie, did the same, bringing the population of the simple frame house to seven, covering four generations, not uncommon for the time. Katherine's other brother, Tennille, married and with a son, Frank, moved to a nearby apartment. Tennille's arrival, along with his family, at the Henderson home for the almost daily family musters would bring the men my father's age in the house to a total of three.

Discipline for my cousins and me was assigned to the adult closest to the child needing the discipline. While this might have diluted authority on some occasions, neither my cousins nor I doubted that authority was always nearby. My uncles might have been more eager to lend a hand, or apply a hand to me, than they would had my father lived. Whether they did so consciously or not, the result was the same: my three uncles were the major male role models in my early life.

Another dilemma for my mother must have been how to evoke my father's life. Before the age of support groups and counselors, self-help books and pop psychology, my mother and over 100,000 other widows were left to figure it out alone. My mother must have known that how she talked about my father and her approach to her loss would shape my life and my ability to cope in his absence. Though I will never know how she handled her loss privately, other than through her writings, what I remember of our talks about him was tenderness and wistfulness.

In my preschool years, my mother would tell me that my father was in heaven and looking down on me. When I noticed the stars in the early evening, she would tell me that the brightest star was a window in heaven through which my father could see me. When we said our prayers at night, he was always named both as a prayer recipient and as a godly attendant who could put in a good word for me. Later, as I learned the Lord's Prayer, I interpreted the opening words to refer to *my* father who art in heaven. I don't remember that she discouraged this.

My mother's faith in God sustained her. Though she attended church regularly during my father's military service, she was more committed to her faith and church after my birth. She now had another life to worry about, and introduc-

Conrad IV and his mother, Christmas 1958.

ing me to religion, her church community, and the basis of faith was one good way to cope with that worry. She would later tell me that God has no grandchildren. She continued as a member of the same Episcopal parish, Christ Episcopal Church, for over half a century, serving in almost every leadership capacity.

Her favorite duty, however, was as a Sunday school teacher for five-year-olds, a position she held for twenty years. She would lead her charges to the children's chapel, which was sized for the five-year-old body. Everything was in reduced proportions, including the altar, pews, and room itself. At some point, my mother felt the altar in this child-sized chapel should have an appropriately sized Christian cross as the central fixture. She donated a brass cross, eight or ten inches high, the inscription on which was in memory of my father. How often would I point this out to my friends as a five-year-old and for many years that followed? This link made him more real. The cross remains in the children's chapel to this day.

Selected totems of my father's life and death gave me reference points to link my life to his. Most prominent in our home was the picture of his P-51 Mustang with my name on the engine cowling, my father beaming beside it, smiling directly at the camera, his two-day beard only adding to the scene's virility. Dozens of other pictures showing his life from preteenage years through his Army training were in the photo albums my mother meticulously maintained. Certificates from a grateful nation and state lamenting his death but confirming his heroism hung in my room to remind me that he had died honorably and bravely. My friends, awestruck, would often comment on them, and at one point I memorized the words:

> In grateful memory of Second Lieutenant Conrad J. Netting who died in the service of his country in the European area, June 10, 1944.
>
> He stands in the unbroken line of patriots who have dared to die that freedom might live, and grow, and increase its blessings. Freedom lives, and through it he lives in a way that humbles the undertakings of most men.
>
> Harry S Truman

Be it known that the State of Texas places the name
of Conrad J. Netting upon the roll of those who have
rendered the highest service. The loss of his life in the
service of his country in World War II will always be
remembered by those who love freedom.

In humble recognition of his sacrifice, the Legislature
of Texas, in the name of its people, has directed me
to acknowledge the debt of free men to him who gave
his life that others might live, and commend him to
the living memory of Texans everywhere.

Coke R. Stevenson

As with every veteran of the war, my father was awarded (post-
humously) the World War II Victory Medal and the World War II
Honorable Lapel Service Button. He also received the Army Good
Conduct Medal. When I wrote to the National Personnel Records
Center in 2003 asking for records of my father's service, they sent me
no records (they had burned in 1973). They did send a new set of all
my father's medals, though I hadn't requested them. I now have two
Purple Hearts, one too many.

Congress, in an act passed on August 1, 1947, authorized lapel
buttons for the next of kin of those in the Armed Forces who lost
their lives during the war. The one-half-inch diameter circular pins
were furnished to surviving widows, parents, and siblings. I never
saw my mother or grandparents wear their pins, though we did find
my mother's among her treasures after she died. Known as the Gold
Star Lapel Button, it consists of a gold star on a purple background
bordered in gold and surrounded by gold laurel leaves. It has the look
of a diminutive Purple Heart medal. My mother's initials are inscribed
on the back.

Field trips to a local museum would always trail past a series of
memorial plaques that held the names of San Antonians who had
died in World War II. Seeing my father's name, the same name as
mine, would give pause to even the most callused bully.

The foremost reminder I had was the United States flag that draped
my father's coffin at his reburial at the Brittany American Cemetery,
St. James, France. This flag was sent to us "as a gesture from a grateful

nation," words that even today bring forth deep emotion. This flag connected me to him in a way that other pieces did not, perhaps because it was so near to him, though in death, not life. The wool flag was rough to the touch. Separately stitched stars, forty-eight of them, dated the flag in later years, but we still flew it proudly on national holidays.

Eventually it became tattered and faded after many cleanings (which were free at our neighborhood cleaners, owned by an East European Jewish immigrant) and from repeated use and exposure to the weather. I had to admit that this most meaningful of flags would never be unfurled again, and determined to have it properly folded and framed in a glass case. As my wife, son, and I discussed this with the frame shop owner, a Japanese American, I asked him to be sure it was folded correctly. He said, "Your father would want his son and grandson to fold it." I was speechless, amazed at the insight of this craftsman. Gathering my memories from my elementary school flag duty days, my son and I folded the flag as well as any military honor guard. The framed flag is displayed in my study today.

I feel a singular link to my father when I sing patriotic songs and hymns. I get extended chills and stand straighter when I recite the Pledge of Allegiance knowing that "liberty for all" was partly secured by my father. Or when I sing "My Country 'Tis of Thee" and get to "land where our fathers died," or, in the fourth verse, "Our fathers' God to thee." Or singing the "National Hymn," which includes references to "God of our fathers." Or singing "America" in the second verse: "O beautiful for heroes proved in liberating strife, who more than self their country loved, and mercy more than life!" To me, these are direct references to my father and his sacrifices, and I am reminded of him every time I sing them in my sometimes on-key tenor voice. In those moments he and I unite.

Other connections came from the many ladies my mother knew whose husbands had died during the war and left fatherless children. Billie Wallinder, my mother's best friend, had a child, Barbara, in 1944, six months after her husband died. These women were supporting each other whether they knew it or not. The children must have supported each other, too, in ways we never recognized. Many of these children and I remained friends into our adult years.

The elemental issue for my mother, though, had to be whether she would remarry and what effect that would have on me. She wrote to me in my twenties:

> Unexpected responsibility and lack of funds forced me to cling to the family. Probably that tremendous psychological trauma frightened me so badly that I was powerless to leave the security of the [family]. [Mama] may have wished that I could have left the family and been the independent adult I never became, despite the strong image I project (but who knows oneself?). I resent the fact that my father never lived with me. Probably a psychiatrist would describe this as a rejection complex.
>
> Perhaps it helped me want to marry the very strong man I found in your father. Perhaps it has interfered with my ability to remarry because I have never found another man strong enough to assume the role of father-husband. Perhaps I have sublimated the strong drive I have always had to remarry by living in the shadow of such strong father figures as [my employers].
>
> Be sure of this, Conrad: for several years after your father's death, I secretly dreamed he was alive and would return – when I finally had to admit he was dead, I longed to marry again. To this moment, I consider marriage the only natural state for the adult human being. God knows what lives within us. He is God, and He always has, does now, and always will understand and forgive us. Only our fellows will stone us.

She did remarry, a year after writing that letter, at age forty-nine.

Research shows that the children of unremarried war widows had many problems not only growing up but also as adults, and perhaps more so as they glimpsed their own mortality. These financial and societal troubles affected them deeply. *Newsweek* reported: "The children whose fathers did not return were left to negotiate their way in the euphoria of postwar America." My mother and I negotiated our way, but no such problems afflicted my home, education, maturity, or personal economics. (Though, to quote my mother again, "Who knows oneself?") Whether good judgment, intellect, chance, or Divine miracle played a part, those issues in any long-lasting form were simply not present in my life.

My mother wrote, "I longed to marry again." Doing so in her twenties or even her thirties would have further suppressed painful memories of her brief time with my father. And she no doubt would not have referred to him without prompting in deference to her new husband. But she did not remarry then, and she did not refer to him very much even when she clearly knew her life might be ending. The subject rarely came up.

For reasons I cannot grasp, I never asked more from my mother or anyone about details of his schooling, career, training, Army service, or health. Perhaps she thought I would ask when I was ready, but I wonder how she felt when I never did. Disappointed? Resigned? Relieved? I'll never know. Or maybe she sent signals to me that her emotions were too tender for that conversation, though I doubt this. Maybe she was trying to forget. And maybe I was too busy worrying about the future and my place in it to ask about the past and my place in it.

On one occasion my mother's emotions did surface. As we were completing a three-week vacation to England, Egypt, and Europe in 1963, we stopped in Paris to make the required visits to the mainstays of Parisian tourism. As planned, we also went to the Brittany American Cemetery, several hours from Paris, to visit my father's grave for the first time. At nineteen, I was not as independent as I wanted to be. With my mother's take-charge personality, I had no need to find that independence on this trip.

My only recollection of our short time at the cemetery is my mother leading the way into the caretaker's office to seek directions to the gravesite. As the deferential manager greeted us and asked for the name of our relative, my mother began crying uncontrollably. Her sobs were so powerful that she had to be seated in the quiet, thread-bare reception room. Though the caretaker was no doubt used to this scene, I wasn't, and it took me a moment to realize that my mother was not going to take charge of this conversation. I gathered my composure and put my arm around my mother and said, "We wish to see the grave of Conrad Netting." The man turned to his locator book, and I continued consoling my mother. Soon she regained her poise and we finished our visit. Later she would remark to friends, "Conrad grew up that day."

On that day my mother also attended the funeral rites that had been denied her in 1944. Here, in a quiet part of Brittany not eighty kilometers from where her husband died, was a cemetery. Not a civilian one with an asymmetrical layout and incongruous markers, but a military one with precision evident in every sightline. Here was a cross, white and pure, solid, unambiguous, and standing for the ages. On the cross was his name, Army serial number, group and squadron, state of birth, and date of death, confirming what my mother had seen only in pictures. And here, under the cross, was his body. She was tangibly reunited, at last, with my father's earthly body. I remember nothing of what we said that day or in the days that followed. Perhaps I don't need to.

If I have one regret about my spiritual link with my father it is this: since I have never spoken to him I have no familiar name for him. Would I have called him Daddy, or later Dad or Pop, or something more personal? He was always referred to in the third person as "your father" or "your dad." I co-opted these references in my own conversations, only occasionally getting stuck saying "Dad did this," or "Dad did that." "Dad" is an endearing name and I feel awkward using it for someone I never met. It is probably a big deal only to me. My children, his grandchildren, had no such qualms. They agreed "Granddad" would be their name for him.

As my mother wrote, she secretly dreamed that he was alive and would return. So did I. Well into my teenage years, before sleep would come, I would manufacture the scene where my father walked in the front door. I worked through the shock, joy, doubt, and embarrassment of his return and moved on to the practical steps I would take: introducing him to my friends, shopping for a car, getting new clothes, and on and on. Sleep would eventually end my woolgathering, though that transition was a most happy time.

What if that one convoy had not attracted his attention that June day? Would he have come home? Would the plans of my parents' youth, "four boys and a goat ranch with a landing strip," have survived with him? Or would my parents have settled into more realistic pursuits? Looking through the long lens of sixty years, several options seem possible.

The South Texas goat ranch scenario would have drawn my father outside, away from pesky phones and confining cubicles. No college degree required. Pursuing his passion for flying would have been easy since the ranch would have ample space for a landing strip. He might have herded his goats by air, calling my mother by radio to say he'd be late for lunch, then doing lazy barrel rolls to pass the time. If, as he said, he couldn't live in the same town with his father, then the ranch would have provided that separation. Soon enough, though, the cost of flying, the age of the pilot, and the uncertain income from goats might have forced him back into town toward a more stable career.

He might have inherited entrepreneurial talent from his Netting gene pool, leading him to pursue a business that would fit his expansive personality. Any sales position would have been instinctive for him, leveraging his broad base of friends into a long list of customers. Again, no college degree required. A starter home in a postwar neighborhood (minus the sidewalks, victims of the concrete shortage after the war), would have soon become too small, assuming the other three boys arrived. He and my mother would have been on the upwardly mobile American spiral enjoyed by legions of returning veterans.

A nascent petroleum career seems less likely partially because to succeed he would have needed a college degree. In none of my father's letters did he speak favorably about either such a career or returning to college, though at that time the G.I. Bill was years away.

The thought of his returning creates too many trails, and I cannot see clearly any one of them. Still, he might have returned, got on with his life, and had his share of good and not so good times. I imagine that his life would have, on balance, seen far more good than not and that he would have in his later years been satisfied with it. Would my parents have discussed the war with me, told me stories of heroes, near misses, friends lost, and periodic reunions? Probably not, as few of that generation talk like that. My parents would have had a covenant about the war: they would keep what they lived through to themselves. Their roles in the war would be private, for them to know and me (and my brothers?) to find out. Their letters would have been tossed out along with many of the keepsakes I now treasure.

I have no doubt that my parents would have loved even more deeply in their dotage than they did in their youth. I regret not being able to witness that.

Randall married my mother's best friend, Billie Wallinder, in 1948. They settled in San Antonio and had a daughter, Susan, in 1952. Randall had a distinguished career designing intricate glass fittings and doors for businesses and homes. He died of a heart attack in 1988.

After Randall married and my great-grandmother and grandparents died, my mother and I continued to live with her brother Jimmie, who never married. As my mother was starting her career, sharing financial responsibilities with him made her life easier. In her forties, however, I suspect she felt her youth had passed. Her only child was grown, college educated with two degrees, and in his own apartment, and yet she had never had a house to call her own, to decorate in her own way, to share with a husband who was committed to her happiness. She once told a friend, "I never cooked a meal for [Conrad]."

And what happened to me? My life, until the footlockers beckoned, had no dramatic variances from the norm. (Of course, having no father was not the norm, but it seemed that way to me.) I became a C.P.A. specializing in family wealth management. Since "Conrad" means, in the old German, bold counsel, I suppose my career was predetermined. I married Pauleen Daunt, the daughter of an Irish Episcopal priest, in 1978. Eventually we had three children: Lesley, Cynthia, and, of course, Conrad J. Netting V. The role I assumed in my family, my career, and my church (the same church my mother attended) was as a steward, careful with what I was given, blessed by the trust of others.

My thoughts about my father or any of my ancestors were sporadic until our footlocker discovery in 1994. On one occasion I detoured while on a business trip to Detroit to meet one of my father's cousins and to see some evidence of my great-grandfather's business in downtown Detroit. On another, while I was in graduate school at Texas A&M University, I would walk my friends past the Memorial Student Center, which held a plaque honoring former students, including my father, who had died in World War II. At times my mother and I would be invited to a party at which her friends would mention my father and some physical similarities between us. But other than these events and a few others, my father rarely entered my consciousness.

For the fiftieth anniversary of D-Day, my church planned a small exhibit of World War II memorabilia and asked members to bring items. I gathered some things from the meager treasures I had at that time and gave them to the coordinator, a retired Army colonel. To no one's surprise, an excess of D-Day materials appeared, culled from the archives of the many retired military officers who were members of our church.

The coordinator asked me to speak to the congregation for a few minutes at the commemorative Sunday service. I did, but I had so little to mention about my father's last flight and Army Air Corps service that I resorted to filling my time with quotations from his memorial certificates. While these were appropriate for the circumstances, they did not reveal much about my father. A month later, the contents of his footlockers would.

———————— ★ ————————

CHAPTER FOURTEEN

A Forgotton Footlocker
Reveals Its Secrets

That day in 1994 didn't start momentously. But as we stood on the patio before my father's second footlocker, everyone was speechless as they studied the contents. There, in the wooden box, amid hundreds of mothballs, were many of my father's treasured possessions from his few months in England. Nervous excitement replaced the silence as we began to understand the extent of our find. Packed with love and sensitivity were his flight log, his medals (Purple Heart, Air Medal), magazines and newspapers, uniforms complete with insignia, folded and ready to be worn, stationery, a desk set, letters, and his military file and debriefing reports. In short, nearly everything that would have been with him in England during those tense days leading up to D-Day. As I drew my hand lightly over the uniform, flight log, and letters, all on the top, I felt I had for the first time touched my father.

Our first thought was that the quartermaster in England had assembled my father's possessions and sent them home. As we surveyed the contents, however, we realized that could not be, or at least not entirely. For in the footlocker were letters from my father to my mother and his posthumous Purple Heart. Although the Army had sent the trunk home, my mother had handled the final packing and included in it what she wanted.

The contents were of her choosing, and so was their arrangement, as if she wanted whoever opened the footlocker to see them in a certain order. On the top left was my father's Army Air Corps blouse, or jacket, folded in half along the breast pocket, with its full set of insignia and ribbons showing. To the right were the medal cases with the large medals inside. His desk set, a folded leather writing kit that included an ink blotter, space for photographs, a calendar, and compartment for stationery, was there. We found his draft card from October 10, 1940. The calendar showing was June 1944 with the tenth carefully circled, another message across the decades from my mother, as if to say, In case you don't remember, you who open this, here is the day my life changed. Next we found the flight log and read aloud two of the debriefing reports my father had written. Written in the colorless language of war, my father on several occasions claimed German planes destroyed, careful not to use the more emotional word "killed," as that might bring emotions to the surface that were best left undisturbed.

My later research revealed that several of my father's possessions were not in the footlocker: his trench coat, neckties, pocketknife, camera, and pipe, among other things. Though I was not disappointed in what we had found, I felt that those additional items would have revealed even more.

By now my family was somber, realizing perhaps that we had opened a symbolic coffin. If so, we soon had much more to be somber about. As I was processing this overload of data and emotions, I realized that we should look in the flight log for June 10, 1944, to see what happened that day. At that point I knew only that my father was killed in France but not under what circumstances.

The dozen relatives surrounding me grew even quieter as I began to read the epitaph Pat Patteeuw had written fifty years before. "Today was Con's last flight" was as far as I got. Gathering my composure, tears welling behind my eyes, I tried again but made no more progress. Realizing that I couldn't go on, my wife, Pauleen, took the log and read the entire entry. Of course, my mother had also read this entry. Under what circumstances? Alone? And when? On arrival or much later? No one knows.

In those spare words, barely one hundred of them, Pat accounted for my father's last flight and memorialized him and his heroism, the heroism he never sought. Pat wrote that my father "flew as an extra," establishing immediately his commitment to duty, his availability, his impatience with sitting around. "In his eagerness to stop an enemy truck convoy" means that, once airborne, he was not shy about finding targets and taking them on. Pat was careful to use delicate language, knowing his friend's widow would read it, so he wrote, "He gave his life."

"Con was . . . leading the rest of the squadron" speaks of leadership, of a take-charge attitude, and of follow-me courage. "While he was firing" tells us he was not only leading but involved. And to remind every reader that my father had no chance of survival, Pat wrote, "[his plane] was seen to crash and explode." Pat continued with a description of my father as "a very good friend" and "a valuable man" and closed by subordinating his feelings to Con's family: "[Our loss] will be nothing as compared to the loss to Katherine and Conjon IV." Apparently, my father had convinced Pat, too, that I would be a boy.

Pat conveyed my father's core personality, the finality of the crash, and how his memory would endure to his friends and family. That we first read such a testimony on Independence Day escaped no one's attention.

At that time we had no connection to the author who had printed the message in a careful hand. Pat's signature was neat but not easily interpreted. Consumed by the power of the message, we took no time to consider the author's connection to my father or why he would have written what he did.

In the following weeks, as I sorted through the treasures from the footlocker, I took the uniforms to a dry cleaner. The store's owner, on seeing what I had brought, passed his hand over the material as if it was the fabric of kings. He said that those uniforms were exactly the ones he had worn and promised to treat them lovingly and respectfully, which he did. I placed the desk and toiletry sets in prominent display in my home and office. But the letters were a problem. They were generally in chronological order by recipient, and to read them for the most understanding I would have to sort them by mailing dates.

Months later, as I unloosed the first ribbon, pale blue, half-inch-wide silk, I was struck that I was invading my parents' privacy. These were, after all, their love letters. They weren't meant for other eyes, even five decades later. I couldn't continue. After several more months, I felt called to try again, this time thinking (rationalizing?) that my mother had put those letters there for a reason. She apparently had no inclination to reread them – she sealed them, after all, in that footlocker. So she must have saved them for someone else, probably me. Had my father lived, I could have heard from them just how devoted they were to each other. Since he did not, weren't these letters a poignant replacement for those unspoken conversations? If so, then they would want me to know, and therefore I should read each one to learn more about them and, by inference, myself.

But what about sharing those private thoughts with others? Did I have the right to do that? Pauleen and I discussed the issue fervently but finally decided I did. Supporting us was Psalm 102:18: "Write down for the coming generation what the Lord has done, so that people not yet born will praise him." Still, I sometimes have misgivings about divulging to the world my parents' private writings. But much of what they wrote needs to be shared in hopes it will help others understand the times and how their families might have acted and reacted. Besides, I have withheld the most private writings, as is appropriate.

I sorted the letters and added other writings and memorabilia I had from my family, both distant and close, resulting in a near perfect plot line from early 1941 through 1946. The only gaps in my parents' writing were when they were together, which was not often or for long. Otherwise the letters serve as a continuum over those crucial years.

On weekends and evenings I sorted and researched. I would remove a letter from its envelope, place each into archival-quality plastic sleeves, and then repeat the process. I did not read the letters as I went along. But the more involved I got with the evidence, the more I wanted to learn. I wanted to know who wrote the epitaph. How could I find him (in pre-Internet days)? How, even, did he spell his last name? One night the thought struck me: if he knew my father in England, maybe he knew him in stateside training!

Energized, I went to the best evidence I had, the record of my father's training class, dubbed 43-I. Looking exactly like a high school annual, the record had a formal head shot of each graduate, a few casual photos, the instructors' names, and a few inside jokes about the class. Under many of the photographs were short messages and signatures of classmates. I could tell the name I was looking for began with P, and there it was: Joseph "Pat" Patteeuw, not a common last name and thus not readily discernable from the signature in the flight log. But on close inspection, the two were the same. And Pat Patteeuw was from Detroit, my father's hometown. Could they have been buddies as far back as Detroit? Never mind that now, because I had the name I needed. Next question: could I find Mr. Patteeuw? Could he be found?

After a few weeks of wondering how I would find him, with no solid approach, I called my cousin Frank Henderson. We had grown up together, played together, and been in mild trouble together as youngsters, and he was now a U.S. Army general at the Pentagon. Frank had been with me when we opened the footlocker, had helped me understand the military insignia, an understanding I could not remember from my own two-year Army career, and had kept a genuine interest in the progress of my research. His respect for his Uncle Con bound us once again, though he had been stationed away from San Antonio for almost three decades.

My request was this: to the extent permissible within Army guidelines, could he try to find what happened to Pat Patteeuw after June 10, 1944? Frank went to work on it. Weeks later, he called to say he had made progress. After spending hours of personal time researching the Pentagon records, he was at a dead end. He mentioned his frustration to his secretary. The man simply was not in the Pentagon records, or at least those records that were accessible. After a brief consideration of this project, she suggested that he call Detroit information. (Yet more evidence of why secretaries run the Pentagon.) On the first try he found a listing for Pat Patteeuw. Calling the number, he reached Pat's brother, who confirmed that Pat was well and living during the winters in Fort Myers, Florida. Frank was given the phone number and urged to call.

But first, Frank called me with the news. I was stunned. He said the rest was up to me. I said that I couldn't just call some eighty-year-old man in Florida and announce that Conrad Netting was on the phone. Pat had seen Conrad die, so he might not think it funny. Convinced that I was right, Frank's secretary called. Pat's wife, Shirley, answered.

The secretary said, "I am calling from the Pentagon for Major General Henderson. He would like to speak to Mr. Pat Patteeuw."

"Okay," said Shirley. Turning to Pat, she said, "Someone's trying to contact you. The Pentagon's on the phone."

"Yeah, some joker," said Pat. He figured it was one of his old friends giving him the business, no doubt having his wife pose as his secretary and putting on a show.

The secretary said, "The general wants to speak to you."

"Yeah, I'm sure he does," Pat said.

Frank said, "This is General Henderson."

Pat said, "You know, general, I'm a bit old for what you people need in a war. I'm sure there are younger people around to do the job. And not only that, I haven't been in the Army for quite a while. I think it would take too long to bring me up to par." Pat was ready to go along with the gag.

"No. No, this is for real."

"In a pig's ear," Pat said.

Then the general said, "Look, did you know someone named Conrad Netting?"

Pat couldn't respond at first, frozen in time and thought. Over the next few minutes as he spoke with Frank, he began to see a past that had been comfortably hidden for decades.

When I called the next evening, Pat said hello in a clipped Midwestern accent, but neither of us could continue for a few moments. Even with the call prearranged we couldn't speak, couldn't bring ourselves to talk about the man who connected us. Resurrecting the memory of Pat's training pal, beloved roommate, and flying partner after fifty years was overpowering. The seconds ticked by.

I tried to understand that on this phone line was the last living person who knew my father well, and who perhaps had spent more time with him than my mother had. This man was the link that would forever bind me to my father's legacy.

After a while the emotions waned, and we began a warm conversation that shortened the five intervening decades. Over the next several months, we exchanged books, photographs, and anecdotes. Though we intended to meet someday, the opportunity didn't immediately arise. I had other research projects brewing. Motivated by the discovery of the footlocker, I planned to retrace my father's military roots in Debden, England, and to visit his grave in St. James, France, though I had yet to read my parents' letters. I felt that my son, then fifteen years old, and I must see my father's base, or what was left of it, and his grave before any more time passed.

Our first stop in London, the summer of 1995, was at St. Paul's Cathedral. Behind the main altar is a chapel dedicated to Americans killed while based in England during World War II. At the chapel's dedication, Dwight D. Eisenhower, Allied Supreme Commander, said: "Here we and all who shall hereafter live in freedom will be reminded that to these men and their comrades we owe a debt to be paid, with grateful remembrance of their sacrifice and with the high resolve that the cause for which they died shall live."

In this chapel is a book of remembrance naming each of those men. The original, a massive volume bound in red leather, is kept pristine under glass. The names are written in calligraphy. An official turns a page a day so that over time every name is exposed to passing observers. A second volume, an exact copy of the first, is less guarded and, on request, can be opened to any page. We saw yet again my father's name registered for the ages.

The next day we had a car and driver take us to Debden, about ten miles southeast of Cambridge. The field was hard to find, obscured by decades of overgrown brush. After circling the area for an hour, we stopped at an official-looking gate to ask directions. As it was, the gate was for the Debden base. A bomb disposal unit occupied the buildings, so our access was restricted. After some conversation, they agreed to let us take a driving tour, but we had to have an officer of the unit accompany us. The somber brick buildings, originally of the Eagle Squadron, then of the 4th Fighter Group, now occupied by the bomb unit, looked untouched. Only the vines, which had crept much farther along the walls, and the trees belied the fifty intervening years.

The runways were not evident, but inquiry revealed they were now separated from the base by a hedgerow. We left the base, drove fifty feet, and entered a dirt path that quickly led to Runway B, unusable during the war and much worse now. Ghosts seemed to float around us, ghosts of the P-51s and of the pilots, as we drove to Runway A (27/09) which meets Runway B almost perpendicularly. Cracks in the pavement were everywhere, preventing any consideration for aircraft but no problem for our rented SUV, a Japanese make, which was beyond ironic. Both runways had noticeable bumps in them, causing me to wonder if they had been there during the war. Later, we learned from Pat Patteeuw that those bumps, resulting from hasty patches after hits from German bombers in 1940, rendered one runway useless and the other a challenge from which to take off. Ammunition bunkers were at the far end of the field, and we looked in them. The silence was so complete that I could almost hear the voices, commotion, and engines from long ago, ghostly now against the pitted pavement.

Our military guide told us the runways were obsolete, which is understandable. What passes for military might one moment becomes memory the next. But his next comment stopped me. "The community uses them for giant flea markets once a month." What a sacrilege, I thought, these revered grounds reduced to a flea market! But the market's purveyors and shoppers had scant link to the original use or little remembrance of what that use produced and would find nothing untoward about their activities. Luckily, we weren't there on flea market day.

As we approached Cambridge, our driver, who had some sense of history, suggested a stop in Saffron-Walden; he had heard of a memorial to American war dead there. After several stops, with no one able to help us find it, we stumbled across it behind a soccer field. At this stage of our research, new memorials were rare, so we were stunned to find one here. Well kept by the villagers, the memorial had my father's name on its wall along with other names of those stationed in the area who had been killed in combat. How odd, I thought, that my mother never mentioned this, if indeed she even knew of it. As we would learn in the coming years, this was just the beginning of what had eluded us.

A few days later we were in France, heading from Paris to Rennes on the high-speed TGV train. From Rennes we drove to St. James. Beyond that small town was the Brittany American Cemetery, resting place for 4,410 men killed in action during World War II.

The twenty-eight acres of gently rolling land had been a dairy farm, an enterprise common to the area. A few years after the war, the American government with permission from the French bought it from its farmer-owner. Thus it became American soil and a proper burial ground for Americans.

A visit to an American military cemetery invokes deep respect. You stand among the graves of young men who did not seek glory, heroism, or immortality but who, in their sacrifice for our liberty, attained all three. The tranquility, orderliness, and untroubled setting console visitors but also mark the chaos, pain, and death of war. The lovingly tended grounds, managed by Americans, seem at first to deny the war, those who died in it, and those who didn't but feel as if a part of them did. Later you realize that the reverent setting honors its residents and their visitors.

My son and I, with the caretaker leading the way, solemnly entered the central mall of the cemetery to see the stark white crosses and Stars of David arrayed before us in gently curving rows, each exactly like the others. The fanlike arrangement lessened the rigidity. As we walked the perimeter of the first section on our left, I sensed an unnatural detachment. I soon realized that the markers' backs were to us, silent and without inscription, almost inhospitable. This is by design, keeping visitors from the distraction of reading the names, getting involved, until they had surveyed the cemetery as a whole. As we made our way farther into the grounds and looked back toward the entrance, the markers began to reveal personal information. Not coincidentally, the front of the markers face west, toward the United States – and home.

The luminescent white markers against the green grass generate more emotion than most people can take. Whether relative or tourist, the visitor becomes a changed person among these heroic young men. At fifteen, my son was perpetual motion on two legs. But in this setting he was surprisingly composed. When we had said our prayers and let our eyes wander to the other crosses, we soon noticed that the dates of death were all within a few weeks of each other – the first weeks of August 1944. Only my father's was earlier. As I mentioned this, Conrad V said, his voice calm, "We can't let this happen again." And there it was: he had noticeably matured in the hour we had been on this consecrated ground, just as I had so many years before. Was my father, his grandfather, responsible for our growth and maturity in his death, just as he would have been in life? Yes, and I am convinced just as effectively.

We posed awkwardly for pictures, asking the caretaker to be our photographer. I thought that Conrads III, IV, and V were together for the first time, two in flesh, one in spirit. The price of war – death – had separated us, but what it bought – freedom – had reunited us.

Our research was bearing fruit. We had the heirlooms from the footlockers, letters between my parents, and a completed pilgrimage to my father's Army base and gravesite. We also learned from the Internet that my father died near Evreux, France, not far from Paris. But at least one source had not been tapped. A visit to Pat Patteeuw would complete the puzzle, at least as we knew it.

Arrangements were made and my son and I arrived in Fort Myers, Florida, in February 1997. From the airport, Pat and Shirley squired us in their Mercury land yacht. They were gracious to a fault, welcoming us as if we had been close friends for a lifetime. After the war, Pat had traded his flying career for a more sedate life as a Sears store manager. After his first wife died, he and Shirley married and settled into a comfortable retirement, taking their winters in Florida and their summers at Houghton Lake, Michigan. They appeared to enjoy each other's company very much.

Though my son and I only stayed one night, we took four suitcases filled with every memory-jogger for Pat I could think of. We took snapshots, letters, medals, Army forms, training annuals, and books. I sensed Pat was delighted to be reminded of distant times and of his youth. From late afternoon until after ten that night, we taped our conversation. As the discussion warmed and I showed him our memorabilia, I realized his memory was sharp, giving us details that were missing from the letters or his rendition of a story that was reported in the letters. He recalled names, places, and events. He remembered Debden and the squadron's daily activities in detail. He confirmed facts and opinions of my father. But mostly he opened his soul. Until then he had been a card-carrying member of the silent generation. With our visit, though, he seemed to hold nothing back.

Most arresting were his comments about distancing himself from other roommates after my father died, and, later, from anyone else. "I don't want to be hurt anymore. I've been hurt enough. I – I've had enough bad times. I've gone through enough things, and I don't want them to do that to me anymore. And I mean I catch hell from my wife. She says 'You're not a very loving person.' And I say, 'No, I guess not.' "

Our conversation began again the next day after church and continued until we had to leave. We had seen Pat for barely twenty-four hours, but I had learned more about my parents from him than from any other living source.

* * *

As if on cue, Michel Grandin was beginning his research as mine was ending. For fifty-plus years, through grief and joy, and from foreign occupation to freedom, Michel kept the memory of Conrad J. In La Ferté-Macé, where Michel and Louisette now lived, and in Saint-Michel-des-Andaines, just three kilometers apart, Michel would see friends from his childhood, and Conrad J., "the American pilot," would seep into conversations. They would discuss the "brave soldier" who had given his life for them. What had they done to thank him?

Decades before, Michel had foraged through the archives at the Saint-Michel-des-Andaines town hall, intent on finding out more about Conrad J. But nothing was there. In the commotion of August 14, 1944, when the Allies liberated the town, the town's officials gave all information about Conrad J., including his last name and serial number, to the first American officer they saw, as they were required to do. The Adjutant-Chief Commandant summarized the information in a memo given to the Americans that was later translated from the French by Carl V. Olson, 2Lt., Quartermaster Corps:

Report of the Adjutant-Chief Commandant
of the La Ferté-Macé Brigade
(Gendarmerie Nationale)

I have the honor to inform you that on the 9th [sic] of June an English plane fell near the town of Saint-Michel-des-Andaines, Orne, sometimes called Pont-Hardi. The aviator . . . carried a visiting card in the name of "Lt. Conrad Netting," and a certain sum of money. I succeeded in keeping this card but the money was taken by a German soldier.

> The body of this aviator is buried in the cemetery of
> Saint-Michel-des-Andaines. The grave is marked by
> a cross which bears the name of the deceased. The
> card of this officer was given on the 14th of August
> 1944 to the first American captain who entered La
> Ferté-Macé.

Over time, this memo would disappear from the town archives. How frustrated Michel would be at this shortsightedness. Still, he had to admit it was a turbulent time, and in their eagerness to welcome the soldiers and give them the necessary records, the memo about the American pilot was lost.

The conversations between the youngsters of 1944, now the elders of 1999, would turn repeatedly to Conrad J. The only war death in their village and they had not honored him, didn't even know his name, how old he was, or where he was from. Shameful, they said, not to treat a brave soldier better than that.

Then, in 1999, something clicked in Michel's mind. Enough of this; talk gets nothing done. He began to poke around. He heard of a nearby town, Flers, which had a public archivist. He heard of the research being done on the Internet. He learned of Les Fleurs de la Mémoire Association and its goal of having each American grave in France attended semiannually by a French family. The sentiment was overwhelming, and as he approached retirement from his carpentry career, he knew he would have a second career in his life: he would find all he could about Conrad J. He summoned his professional skills of patience, thoroughness, and a desire for everything to fit together, and started his research.

With my research seemingly completed and with the adventure into the past finished, I thought I knew all I could about my parents and their relationship. Though both were dead, they seemed reborn as I vicariously relived their courtship, engagement, marriage and wartime separation, and my father's death. Perhaps I knew my mother better than when she was alive, an embarrassing thought. As I finished cataloging their letters, filling eleven three-inch, three-ring binders, and as the twentieth century closed, complacency ruled.

Emphasizing the footlocker discovery, I made several speeches around San Antonio to civic clubs and churches. After that, with nothing new to keep the story fresh, I put it aside as if finishing a good book. But to some it was an incomplete book. Pat Patteeuw said, during our interview, "You don't have a climactic ending." I said, "Maybe it just needs to say it's the end, the loose ends were tied up. And maybe this weekend [with you] is the ending. To round out the letters I have with the firsthand knowledge you have completes the story. I don't know what else needs to be done."

Not that I had much time to do anything else about it. For five years after that interview, Pauleen and I were living life on fast forward. Conrad V graduated high school and entered college, making "empty nest" more than just a catch phrase. Cynthia graduated from Texas A&M, her grandfather's and my alma mater, and within a few months she was diagnosed with Hodgkin's disease. She required chemotherapy treatments for six months. With her cancer in remission, she married a college sweetheart who was in the Army and moved with him to Hawaii. Lesley, who had married in 1994, had, over the five years after the interview, two children, our grandchildren, as she and her husband began careers. My firm moved from downtown followed by a partner separation. And Pauleen and I sold our home of twenty years and moved nearby into a smaller home requiring fewer responsibilities. My third neck surgery soon followed.

With all of that, there wasn't time left to further develop my parents' story.

CHAPTER FIFTEEN

──────── ✭ ────────

A Large Envelope from France

The mail that February afternoon sat on our kitchen counter. I skimmed through standard pieces until the envelope was the only one left. As Pauleen finished in the kitchen, I opened it, noting the Paris return address, and found a pile of documents and a handwritten letter. I began to read.

January 28, 2002

Dear Sir:

> *First of all, I would like to apologize for bothering you. We hope you are the one who could help us.*
>
> *My father is looking for more information about a brave soldier called Conrad J. Netting, killed in action, during the Second World War in Normandy and buried in France.*
>
> *We hope you are maybe his son, or his nephew, or next to him.*
>
> *You will find enclosed some documents and letters to show you the research my father has done on Mister Netting.*
>
> *It is so important for my father who asked a few months ago for a memorial to be built in Saint-Michel-des-Andaines (place of death). The memorial is built now and they don't even know Conrad J. Netting's date of birth.*
>
> *My father would also like to get a picture.*
>
> *Many thanks for helping us.*

> *Best regards,*
> *P/O Michel Grandin*
> *His daughter S. Grandin*

Pauleen asked about the contents, but I could hardly speak. Was this someone's demented joke? After muttering something about crackpot hoaxes, I turned to the second page, which was more formal, typed, and addressed to the U.S. Army.

August 17, 2001

Dear Sir,

I would like to have some information about a soldier killed in action during WWII and buried in France, in the Brittany American Cemetery – Saint James.

> *Name: Conrad J. Netting*
> *Army serial: 0694174*
> *Unit: 336 Ftr Sq, 4 Ftr Gp*
> *Date of death: 10 June 1944*
> *Place of death: Saint-Michel-des-Andaines*
> *(61/Orne France)*

My father, who was a cabinetmaker, made the casket for this brave soldier's burial. (I was a little boy, eleven years old, and with all my family we went to the funeral, I will never forget it.) We are so grateful to this young man for fighting for a land that was not his own, and so sorry that he died far away from his homeland.

This is one of the reasons why I want to know more about the soldier Conrad J. Netting, and I also belong to Les Fleurs de la Mémoire Association. I regularly visit the tomb and lay flowers on it, paying tribute to this soldier fallen to liberate my country. I would be very thankful to you if I could know more about this short life.

Sincerely yours,
M. Grandin

The surge of emotions was too much for me. I got to the second paragraph, then couldn't continue, then couldn't stand. Pauleen said later that my face turned white and my legs seemed to crumple as I collapsed into a nearby chair. She read the letter, then grew pale herself. What did we have here? No joke, for sure, since no one could make this up.

My mind was spinning. Could my father, whom I thought had crashed with nothing left to bury, have been so respectfully, lovingly, and tenderly cared for? Just a few years earlier, when I interviewed Pat Patteeuw, he said, "I checked with the intelligence officer, say maybe about July 15 [1944]. He said some farmer came by right after to see if he could salvage anything." I was pleasantly shocked then to know that within a month whatever remained had been found. Pat continued, "They knew immediately. Anybody within a radius of miles would have heard and seen [the explosion]." He was right.

Incredulous, I turned to the next page, an official-looking U.S. Army form titled "Disinterment Directive." On it was the official Graves Registration account of moving my father's body from Gorron, France, to St. James. For years I had known only that he was buried at St. James. Just moments ago I had learned from Michel Grandin that he was buried in Saint-Michel-des-Andaines. Now I read that it was Gorron. The form was explicit about the "condition of remains," the details of which I hope to forget someday.

The next piece in the stack was a computer-drawn color picture of someone's recollection of the crash. It meshed precisely with Pat Patteeuw's description in the flight log.

I believe that I went into some mild form of mental shock. I simply couldn't process all that I had read. I tried to focus my mind, then noticed that Pauleen was reading the documents as well. Though more controlled, she, too, was on the verge of incredulousness. As we grappled with what we had read, we barked out exclamations and questions. Who is S. Grandin? Who is M. Grandin? How could they get all this data? How did they ever find us? This is crazy! Who would believe it? And on and on.

Though the facts of my father's death were finally before us and presumably correct, the big question shifted from what had happened after the crash to how we could contact this family, and how much more they knew. Within an hour we were on the Internet, using our meager skills in that medium to link the return address with a phone number. After many false starts, dead ends, and failures, some hours later we got to the address. Then we found that it was an apartment with dozens of names, none of them Grandin. Frustrated, we finally made a link between S. Grandin and her married name, S. Grandin-Nicolle. After more halting Internet research, we produced a phone number to associate with S. Grandin-Nicolle. Calling Paris is not something I do regularly, so then we had to figure out how to make such a call. Finally, with a presumably valid phone number, we made one more Internet search: the time difference between San Antonio and Paris. The gap was seven hours. By now it was well after midnight in France. We would have to wait.

That night I slept little, though I don't recall my specific thoughts. Generally, I was thinking of my father, his last moments, and this Norman family who had found us. I wondered where this would lead. This day had become a turning point in my life. What was the date, I wondered, so I could remember? Oh, yes, February 2 – 02/02/02.

At church the next day we told no one, still unsure of what we could say or should say. It was too extraordinary to understand ourselves, let alone convey to others. After a desultory lunch, I picked up the phone and dialed.

Sylvie Grandin answered and, I quickly learned, spoke exemplary English. She said she was so happy, just thrilled, to get my call. I told her I was thrilled, too, but she dismissed that, not rudely but firmly. She began speaking about the papers she had sent, how long she and her father had been looking for the Netting family, and how overjoyed she was to hear from me. Again I tried to say it was I who was thrilled. Imagine, I said, how I felt to know that my father had been treated so lovingly at his death. She insisted that it was they who were honored.

"Who asked your grandfather to make the coffin?" I asked.

"No one," she said. "He wanted to do it to honor this brave soldier."

"How many coffins did he make for Americans during the war?"

"This was the only one."

I asked about the monument her father wanted built. She said he was intent on completing it and, after many delays, had gotten permission.

"How many other names will be on it?"

"Only Conrad J. Netting."

Her only question of me? My father's birth date. I gave it to her: June 7, 1918.

Every time she spoke she reiterated how honored they were that I had called. I tried to insist that it was I who was deeply honored. She would have none of it.

I asked about the tomb that her father visited twice annually. "How many bodies are in it?"

"Only one, your father." I realized that "tomb" to her was a "grave" to me.

"You mean *your* father visits *my* father's grave twice a year?"

"Yes."

"Why?"

"Because he feels he has lost a brother, or a son . . . no, a brother."

I promised to send pictures of my father and my family. She said her father would be so happy. She promised to send more information that her father had about the crash and the funeral.

"How many Americans were killed in the village?" I asked.

"Only one. Your father."

"Who drew the computer-generated picture?"

"A friend drew it from my father's recollection."

I told her how flattered I was that her father was so thoughtful toward my father. She inhaled deeply and said sternly that I still didn't understand.

"Look at the computer picture and notice the two German trucks. They were carrying fuel as their cargo and were going to destroy or help destroy the French. Your father," she explained, "blew up the trucks before they could do so. How could the town, and my father in particular, not be forever in debt to your father?"

I was speechless.

She continued, saying that because of this brave soldier, Normans survived and her father would never forget it, him, or what he did. "We proud Normans are the ones who owe honor and thanks for what your father did."

After about forty-five minutes, we reluctantly brought the conversation to a close. She said she would call her father immediately and tell him this news. "He will be so happy!"

No happier than I.

The next day an e-mail arrived from Sylvie, who said she had called her father to tell him the news. She wrote, "You cannot even imagine how my father was overcome and happy. He said, 'Oh, my God, his son, his son, he has a son. Mr. Conrad J. Netting has a son. That's wonderful. I cannot believe it!' "

He told her again about the crash and the subsequent events. She wrote, "My father said that the Germans were more crazy than ever four days after D-Day. My father said that my grandfather ran with some neighbors just by the place of the crash, to help the pilot (your father), but unfortunately it was too late." She then added the most satisfying words I could have read, even though she had translated them from French. She wrote, "My grandfather took care of your father." *Took care of.* Three simple words that will forever define how these guileless Normans put their own safety aside, ignored their enemy, and acted on behalf of one who needed help. But, after all, hadn't my father done all three for them?

These words were a code for what happened that day, events too graphic to mention. I could easily imagine what Louis Grandin had seen after the crash and explosion, what he and the others had smelled in the spent kerosene, and what they had touched. There was nothing else to say.

Sylvie, at thirty-nine, was the first generation in her family not to know World War II firsthand. Being one generation removed gave her a distance from the emotions and heartbreak that her parents and grandparents had felt. Even so, she was aware of what was at stake during the war. She wrote, "As I told you, I'm very proud to be Norman and French, and I am really grateful and thankful to your father and also to all the brave young American, Canadian, [and other Allied] soldiers fallen to liberate our country."

A week later, on February 10, another of Sylvie's e-mails added to our rapidly increasing knowledge. "About the memorial. My father wanted to make a photograph of it, but he was not allowed yet. The Mayor of Saint-Michel-des-Andaines said that he has to wait for the official commemoration in March or April." In her close, she sought to secure the tenuous link we had made. "We really hope to keep in touch with you and to meet you one day."

By late February Sylvie had mailed us another packet of documents and pictures. The latter included our first look at the Grandin family, ranging from a picture of Louis taken in about 1952 to one of Sylvie's wedding in 1998 with all her family shown in it. Other photos showed my father's cross at St. James and the cemetery at Saint-Michel-des-Andaines.

I sent the Grandins photos of my family, including six or eight of my father in the months just before his death. I included a copy of the most cherished one, of him and his plane with my nickname "Conjon IV" boldly lettered on the engine cowl. As I prepared the photos for mailing, I thought how disquieting these pictures might be for the Grandins. Over the decades they probably formed an image in their minds of my father's appearance – his features, his size, his frame. I wondered how close their mental image was to reality. I also sent a photocopy of the epitaph Pat Patteeuw had written in my father's flight log.

Though so much was developing so quickly, I kept my eye on one event: the dedication of the memorial in March or April. My C.P.A. business could not do without me at that time of year, but I was adamant that I be there at the dedication. On the off chance the date was flexible, I e-mailed Sylvie in mid-February saying that we would have to miss the dedication. Then I asked if she and her family would be available to meet with us in early June. Her reply did not mention the dedication, only that early June would be fine with them for our first meeting. For two weeks I stewed about missing the dedication, and then I wrote bluntly, "I want to be in Saint-Michel-des-Andaines for the dedication of the memorial plaque. If the dedication could wait until June, then I would be very happy."

Sylvie wrote back, "Don't worry about the dedication of the memorial. I will check with the Mayor of Saint-Michel-des-Andaines. We think that they can wait for you. We'll do our best." Sylvie wrote on March 10 that the dedication would wait for our arrival. Big relief.

In late April, an e-mail arrived from Claude Lavieille, who represents Les Fleurs de la Mémoire Association, the group formed to encourage visitors to the American military cemeteries. At the Colleville and St. James cemeteries, after only one year's effort, the association had arranged for 2,450 graves to be adopted. Claude asked if, when I came to Normandy, I would meet with "the journalists" to tell them my father's story. I said yes.

Leaving any of our family behind was inconceivable. On reflection, though, Pauleen and I felt that our two grandchildren, then ages four and two, were too young. So we made arrangements to take Lesley and her husband, Jason, Cynthia and her husband, Jake, and our son, Conrad V. All we had to do was wait and give thanks for the exceptional blessings God had given us.

———————— ★ ————————

CHAPTER SIXTEEN

Meeting the Grandins

Another mile to the north and I could have seen them. As the plane descended on the final approach to Paris, we were directly over the D-Day beaches. And it was June 6. Surely the pilot would give us a look. But no, the plane's computer was in control of our flight plan, and June 6 or not we wouldn't get to see the beaches.

I do not sleep on overnight flights, try though I might, so for six or seven hours I was left to my thoughts. It was a "pinch myself" kind of reverie, as I tried to grasp how outlandish my position would have seemed six months before. Going to Normandy – seven of us! World War II memorials. Caskets and carpenters. All simply unfathomable. What would the French family be like? Would we be compatible?

As these thoughts bounced around in my head, I found myself transfixed by the small video screen at my upgraded seat. I chose a channel showing a computer-generated graphic of the flight's trajectory as it made its way from Texas over Greenland, to Paris. Just after dawn, as we were approaching Paris from the west and flying directly over those infamous beaches, I tried to relax. Everything would be all right, God willing.

Uneventful landings are my favorite kind, and this one was no exception. With bags under our arms, we staggered through customs, car rentals, breakfast/lunch, and de Gaulle airport's muddle of roads. Once on the superhighways in the countryside, I could relax a little.

I reflected on why God had picked me to receive these revelations. Wouldn't my mother and grandparents, aunts and uncles have cherished these disclosures? Wouldn't this news have brought healing and relief to them? Surely. But maybe the graphic details of the condition of my father's body would have been devastating to those who knew him. Maybe God was, in His perfect timing, waiting for someone just slightly removed to receive the news. My role was conduit and steward, the bearer of news and the protector of its message, a role that would keep me from center stage where I didn't belong.

After driving for six hours, we arrived at our hotel in Bagnoles de l'Orne, two kilometers from Saint-Michel-des-Andaines. A three- or four-acre lake dominated the city's center, giving it the look of an Alpine village, minus the mountains. The Andaines forest, with tall slender trees like sentinels, surrounded the city. Our hotel, just on the edge of town, had been occupied by the Germans during the war and was now a mini-resort for French tourists. The quiet settled on us like a blanket. From our hotel windows, we saw cows in every hedgerow-lined field and flowers in every yard.

Though we had allocated an hour for a nap, I spent the time considering our meeting with the Grandins that evening. What would they be like? And how would I stay awake? After dinner, about 10 p.m., we walked in the garden by the parking lot, waiting for our French connection to arrive. In summer, daylight lingers until almost eleven, another assault on our internal clocks. We had been awake for thirty-six hours. Adrenalin was our friend. Then we heard the car and footsteps on the gravel, and we went to meet those who had held my father's memory aloft for fifty-eight years.

The Grandins, with their daughter Sylvie and a friend, Christiane Gillette, both bilingual, made their way toward us. Our greetings were awkward – handshakes or hugs? French or English? The French offer two hugs with air kisses; handshakes are secondary. Amid hellos and chatter, we made our way to the hotel lounge. At this late hour, we were the only customers. A bay window held a semicircular padded window seat large enough to hold four – Sylvie, me, Michel, and Louisette. The others pulled up chairs from nearby tables.

The four of them were more warm, gracious, and genuine than we could have ever expected. Everyone in the group, eleven now, seemed to be on-the-spot friends.

Michel was smaller than I imagined, maybe 5' 7" and slender. Gone was the James Dean look of the 1950s. He was slightly stooped, his silvery hair receding into one impressive wave. He had a pencil mustache. His watery blue eyes betrayed his every emotion. He had much to process. He had just met the son and family of the "brave soldier" who, in town legend, had saved them from destruction.

Louisette, a few years younger, was always near Michel, more supportive than protective. Her voice was mellow, a half octave lower than expected. Her hair, soft and wavy in a Rita Hayworth-style and lightened to a strawberry blond, reached below her shoulders and framed her pale skin.

Christiane Gillette, one of our voluntary interpreters, was a bit younger, and almost elegantly dressed. She looked far younger than her years, and worldly and educated. Though her American husband was now deceased, she had lived with him in the United States for twenty years, returning to her native France years ago. She was intelligent, cordial, and supportive of the Grandins. She was a delight to know and generous to help us.

Sylvie, taller than her parents, was angular and lean, with cinnamon-colored hair cut to neck length, an ear-to-ear smile, and a warmth we could not miss. Her facial features mirrored her mother's. She was stylish, devilish, self-assured, and loyal to her family – though she could dish out a barb or two.

We were barely past an opening sentence or two when Michel handed me something. It was a dossier he had compiled of official war records from my father's file, obtained under the Freedom of Information Act. Inside a cover of robin's egg blue with a small cloth American flag, seventy-two pages contained staggering details. On page one was an 8-by-10 photo of my father in 1942 looking his youthful best, wearing a full smile – almost a laugh – and in his uniform. Little did I know when we sent the Grandins a few small snapshots that they would return this one to us in such a memorable way.

To my mind the central character in this drama, other than my father, was Michel. His efforts, his passion, and, in a sense, his life were tied up in this first meeting. If it failed, he had failed. His eyes darted from person to person, at once seeking approval and getting satisfaction.

Later, Pauleen wrote: "At our first meeting we had time to hear about each other. We were all cautious, nervous, excited, and emotional. I was nervous that the Grandins' concern for Conrad III (and IV) would not be genuine. Later, when I saw how genuine they were,

I was sorry I had felt that way. A lot of time, care, and pride went into gathering all the papers and pictures for the blue binder. Mr. Grandin was eager to see how it was received. He was happy to see in all of our eyes how thankful we were."

Our new friends were cordial, full of smiles and taking our measure. As I looked through the material, commenting on each page, Michel seemed luminous, ready to bust with pride. He turned to me often as he listened or talked. Was he assessing me? Or, having already assessed me, was he seeking my approval? By the end of the evening, both Michel and Louisette seemed relieved. Now we were family.

The next morning we drove to La Ferté-Macé, a few minutes from our hotel. After only one wrong turn and a few laps around the town circle, we found the Grandins' home. We were told to expect "the journalists" there. I imagined a reporter or two from the weekly newspaper to dutifully record the travels of an American family. Again I underestimated Michel Grandin and the force of Les Fleurs de la Mémoire Association.

The Grandin home was modest and modern, finished in stucco painted the color of sand. The neighborhood, fifteen to twenty years old, reminded me of a planned development on an American golf course where the houses are similar but not identical. Each was compact, dominated a quarter-acre of land, and whispered retirement. The temperate climate supported healthy plants laden with color, an unfamiliar sight to our South Texas eyes. The jade-colored grass in the front provided the backdrop. The garden in the back was arresting – plants of every description, some with showy flowers, others with vegetables, and even fruit trees. A rose-covered trellis framed the entry.

The house felt just right. I was surprised that this couple, now almost seventy years old, left their traditional home for a new model with modern conveniences. Downsizing in Normandy?

Once inside the house, we were in a humble combination living and dining room crammed with people. I saw the Grandins, Christiane Gillette, and Sylvie almost immediately. But who were all the other people, at least two dozen, talking loudly enough to make reasonable conversation impossible? English and French mixed without boundaries, an international cocktail party at 10 a.m. The small rooms brought everyone close together. Formal introductions were difficult, so we self-introduced.

We then realized that most of the others were journalists, maybe a dozen strong. Most seemed to be seasoned professionals on the trail of a feature story their viewers and readers would relish. My first impromptu interview was with a baby-faced radio reporter. His portable microphone, close enough for me to swallow, recorded my answers to his expected questions: Are you excited? How do you feel? Are the Grandins all you expected? I responded with benign answers, and after one or two exchanges he ambled away. I never heard if that brief dialogue made it to the airwaves.

Next, a television crew – one man with a bulky camera, the other with notepad and overhead microphone – squeezed up and attempted some questions in English. Though sincere, they couldn't get their point across, and I fumbled an apology about my shortcomings with the French language. Within seconds, a lady appeared beside me and rattled off a paragraph or two in French.

As the crew began to prep their equipment, she introduced herself as Marie Lavieille, the wife of Claude Lavieille, coordinator of Les Fleurs de la Mémoire Association for this area of France. I recalled that Mr. Lavieille had invited me to this meeting with the journalists. Clearly he and his wife were central to this gathering. His limited English meant I spoke mostly with her, and she had plenty to say.

Frustrated with the cramped quarters, Marie signaled the crew and me to follow her to the garden. Once there, we began a more relaxed interview, though it suffered from my language barrier. The men, perhaps in their early fifties, were genial and polite as they directed their questions in French to Marie, who then relayed them to me in English. Though this was extremely awkward, everyone seemed to adapt to the rhythm as the video camera captured the scene. I saw the men's eyes soften as Marie interpreted my comments about my father's actions during the war.

I was struggling to appear relaxed, as if I were interviewed every day. The questions focused on the crash and recovery, a subject I knew well. Still, I wanted my answers to be succinct, so I was concentrating mightily. Then, during one of my illuminating answers, the cameraman sneezed, sending the camera lens pointing toward the damp grass. As if in a trance, I continued until everyone was laughing. I had to laugh, too. From that moment on, I was more relaxed, and the crew seemed to have struck a bond with me that lasted the morning.

As we finished, here came ten or fifteen people around the sidewalk, herded by another reporter and several photographers. They photographed us, Normans and Texans, stretched out single file and grinning for posterity. We later saw that the local newspapers coordinated this amateur photo-op. The pictures appeared in the daily and weekly newspapers, along with detailed stories about my family.

Though I don't recall speaking with any reporters, the articles that appeared were obviously written by professionals. One story had the headline: "The son of the pilot and the son of the woodworker." The article began, "This is not a fable, but a true story." The writer must have had trouble believing the chain of events, and knew that the readers would, too.

We wished we could absorb everything more slowly, to enjoy it more as it unfolded. But that wasn't an option. Pauleen wrote: "The journalists' meeting was overwhelming. I was trying to listen to

---

Saint-Michel-des-Andaines nestles in a slight valley. This view, in 2002, is down the road that fifty-eight years earlier carried the German Army convoy successfully strafed by Lieutenant Netting before his fatal crash.

DELAYED LEGACY

everything and to enjoy what I was hearing. I spent so much time listening that I didn't have time to feel emotions and just 'be in the moment.' I wish I could do it all again and take in more." She spoke for us all.

As if on cue, the hosts and journalists suggested a short trip to see, from a distance, the area where the events of June 10 occurred. Apparently if we got too close we would see the memorial, and they didn't want us to see that until the ceremony the following afternoon. We caravanned to a knoll between La Ferté-Macé and Saint-Michel-des-Andaines.

From there we could see the village of Saint-Michel-des-Andaines, the cemetery, and the busy road that had carried the German fuel trucks. I felt I was in a time warp, though the road noises we heard were not P-51s but Fiats. Perpendicular to the road was a one-lane service road to a nearby home. We assembled on that gravel road to survey the glen below. We gravitated into small groups with a native, an American, and a translator in each. My group included Michel Grandin and Marie Lavieille and was shadowed by the TV crew I had grown to like. With a handheld boom microphone overhead and the camera whirring, Michel described the fighting on June 10, 1944.

I was wholly familiar with the events of that day but unfamiliar with the setting other than through rough drawings. On the morning of the battle the cacophonous guns, engines, and explosions, though lasting only a minute or two, sent civilians scattering for cover. As Michel described the approach of the planes and the position of the trucks, I tried to comprehend how the battle developed. I couldn't grasp how so much could happen in such a confined area. From the road to the crash site it was maybe 300 meters, and in between was the cemetery. In barely the length of a football field trucks exploded, a plane crashed, and my father died.

Weeks later we reviewed photographs of Michel gesticulating as he described the scene. In one, we noticed that the cameraman, the same one who had sneezed during our taping, had turned off his camera and was as absorbed as I was in the description. His close-cut gray hair suggested he was old enough to respect this story but too young to have been alive in those terrible years. With his index finger to his lips, his eyes were on the cemetery a half-kilometer away. This is my favorite photograph from the trip because it suggests just how engrossing the story is. As Pauleen later wrote: "The camera crew was there to do their job. But, as the day went on they became increasingly interested and did not leave for a long time. That is how our story affects everyone. It touches everyone."

After under an hour, we returned to the Grandins' for refreshments and conversation. Several journalists had not returned, so we had more room and less noise. My TV crew, though, was there and asked me off-the-record questions in halting English. Their continued amazement at what they were hearing was evident.

Louisette Grandin served sandwiches. From a round bread loaf she had removed the insides. Slicing that as thin as a wafer, she added butter, ham, and other fillings between two pieces. This contribution of hers was just as lovingly done as what Michel had contributed, and I was grateful for her support.

Mr. Grandin appeared with two bottles of French champagne. He opened one with a flourish and poured, and he and I wordlessly toasted each other with the television cameras rolling.

A while later, Sylvie suggested lunch. We convoyed into La Ferté-Macé. Our numbers traumatized the café owner, who quickly recovered and set up a table for fifteen, far more places than all the other customers combined.

After lunch, some of us toured Mr. Grandin's basement workshop. Evidence of his career was obvious. Large shop machines, well-worn tools (were they inherited from his father?), and a sheer coating of dust left no doubt that Michel's lifetime trade continued as a retirement hobby. As he walked around the well-organized room, he beamed. His mementos lined the walls. Pride lined his face.

From our first contact with the Grandins in February 2002, my primary intention had been to meet and interview Michel Grandin. While the surrounding events would be cathartic, nothing but an interview with Michel would cut to the heart of what I wanted. How much could he remember after almost sixty years, and how much could I rely on? No doubt his memory was augmented by the official documents he obtained. Still, he was the only source I knew of to recall from the French perspective the fearsome events of June 1944.

Conrad Netting IV, right, in the Grandin home in France
in 2002 beside Michel Grandin, son of the carpenter
who secretly built Netting's father's coffin. At the
left is Michel Grandin's daughter, Sylvie.

Our numbers had dwindled to the three Grandins, Christiane
Gillette, and the Nettings. As we gathered in the Grandins' living
room, I was struck by Michel's woodworking pieces, displayed as art.
Two peach-colored roses as big as coasters were on the coffee table,
enhancing the warmth of the wood. On the wall behind the sofa,
Michel had assembled into one frame all the pictures of my family
I had sent months before. The collage had taken effort and some
expense to create, but it brought into his living room the pilot he had
imagined for so long. These mementos told me more about the man
than he could ever say.

Michel and I sat side-by-side on his old-style, smallish sofa. Sylvie
was to his right and Christiane to my left, and both were poised to
interpret. The others sat at the perimeter of the two small rooms.
The seating arrangement, the interpreters, and our new relationship
should have created an insurmountable formality. But everyone was
determined that formalities be overcome. Michel's answers were
honest and unembellished. I remembered, though, that he was recall-
ing events of decades before and allowed him some leeway.

Again, he answered as much with his eyes as his words. He sought my reaction to his answers to see if I would be emotional or unbelieving. I was unemotional given our video cameras, manned by our sons-in-law, and given the few minutes' lapse between each question and its answer.

At times, Louisette supplied remarks, for which I was grateful. With Sylvie translating, however, I was never sure she was giving us the full answer. Christiane was a more direct translator, and sometimes I turned to her for an amplified answer.

I most wanted to know how and when Michel started his research on my father.

Sylvie, translating for her father: "My mother and father in 1999 wanted to research your father's crash. When they asked at the Brittany American Cemetery for your father, the caretaker said he was buried there."

> Q. Did he remember my father's name for all that
> time, or was he reminded of the name in 1999?
> A. He remembered only Conrad J. He didn't know the
> last name, Netting. It was just Conrad J. from 1944
> until 1999.
>
> Q. So did the caretaker find the name Netting?
> A. The caretaker took the first name, Conrad J., and
> said, Okay, we're going to look for it. Then he
> said, Yes, we have exactly what you're looking for.
> Conrad J. Netting. The date of death was the same
> as the crash date.
>
> Q. So the first time your father heard Netting was in
> 1999 at St. James, from the caretaker?
> A. Yes.
>
> Q. How did he feel when he made the connection?
> A. He was so excited. He was so satisfied. He didn't
> quite believe it in the beginning. He wanted to
> know your father's age and to meet his family.
> It was a kind of connection to the past but also
> a search into the future.

Q. Why did he wait until 1999 to start his research?

A. He thought your father was taken back to the United States, but he was still in France.

Q. So something had to click in 1999 to get him interested in writing all these letters. Was there one moment or one event that caused him to start?

A. He heard of others starting research so he felt it would be possible for him to do the same.

Q. How did you connect Netting to me in San Antonio?

A. He wanted me to search the Internet. On one letter [from the Army] was the address of your mother [in San Antonio]. So I saw your name on the Internet in San Antonio. I didn't know if it was the right family.

On just such slender notions – go to a cemetery, ask a question – are lives changed.

I wanted to know how Michel obtained so much material from the U.S. Army, far more than would be normal for such a request. He said, through Sylvie, that he would write three or four times and wait six months for an answer. He began requesting papers in 1999, and then continued to write because he truly wanted to know.

In time, he handed me a summary prepared by the government of Saint-Michel-des-Andaines of how the memorial came to be. "Many older inhabitants of Saint-Michel-des-Andaines, who were teenagers in the 1940s and experienced those turbulent times, have wanted the town to commemorate the death of the American pilot with a plaque. Even though the event occurred more than fifty years ago, it is hoped that this generous gesture will come to fruition this year. A commemorative plaque has been recently provided."

The interview continued successfully though awkwardly for over three hours. The Grandins answered every question, and the interview achieved every objective I sought. I also learned some details I hadn't expected.

Michel volunteered: "The Germans one night got into our cellar to drink cider and take things, things they would take back with them to Germany.

"When the German soldiers heard the Americans were coming [after D-Day], they got drunk. . . . They went shooting at anything that moved. And one German soldier went up in our apple trees . . . waiting for the Americans so he could shoot at them. They went wild. They knew they had lost the war. They had nothing [else] to lose."

The Brittany American Cemetery

Nothing – not the opening scene in *Saving Private Ryan*, not the photographs, not the newscasts of dignitaries on solemn occasions – can prepare you for a visit to a national cemetery, especially one overseas. Whether you have a link to anyone in the cemetery is immaterial. The solemn setting and the sanctity of the sacrifice fill your mind, slow your step, and still your voice until you are forced to acknowledge what lies before you.

> O beautiful for heroes proved in liberating strife,
> who more than self their country loved,
> and mercy more than life!
>
> America! America! God mend thine every flaw,
> confirm thy soul in self-control, thy liberty in law.
>
> *– America*

Pauleen wrote: "Even though I had seen the cemetery pictures and Conrad has told me about what he saw and felt, you have to go and experience the feeling in person. First is the beauty of the cemetery. Green, lush, holy. You automatically become quiet. As we walk to the grave, past so many crosses, the feeling becomes stronger. Our emotions are on the surface."

In an article on the Brittany American Cemetery, Christopher Scanlan wrote, "[The] 4,410 white crosses and Stars of David [are] lined up on a manicured field like a marching band at half time." This would please my father since Texas A&M's marching band is acclaimed for its precision, military origins, and spirit.

Imagine how those thousands of graves came to be in one beautiful place. John Keegan wrote in *Six Armies in Normandy*: "There was . . . work of reparation to be done; the gathering in of the bodies of the soldiers who had died in Normandy's fields and orchards. Buried where they had fallen in the ten weeks of fighting, or thrown together in the mass graves into which the victims of the Falaise pocket were heaped, in the years after the departure of the armies they were disinterred and brought together into more fitting places."

Military documents have allowed us to piece together the journeys my father's body took. First, of course, he was buried in Saint-Michel-des-Andaines cemetery on June 11, 1944. The Allies retook Normandy on August 19, and coincidentally on that date a temporary military cemetery was created in Gorron, a speck of a town some thirty kilometers from Saint-Michel-des-Andaines. In September 1944, my father's body was buried at Gorron along with Allied bodies from all over Normandy. (He was then officially called "remains X-57" despite the dog tags delivered to the Army by the deputy mayor.) His body remained there until February 8, 1949, when he was interred in the cemetery at St. James. The Gorron cemetery continued in service until the last Allied bodies were sent home or reinterred in their respective national cemeteries.

As I learned of this funereal pilgrimage, I thought of 2 Timothy 4:7. We have used it so often in my family at burials, and it was singularly appropriate in my father's case: "I have fought a good fight, I have finished my course, I have kept the faith."

Now, as we walked deeper into the cemetery, with the assistant caretaker in the lead, we followed the same path my son and I had taken seven years earlier. The grass invokes the green of Ireland, owing to the balmy spring weather. However, no matter what the season, the five types of grass, each chosen for its predominate season, assure visitors of a green background for the pearl-white markers. Hundreds of trees – giant Sequoia, white fir, scotch pine, and European oak and elm – frame the graves. But they were less majestic than on our earlier visit; a devastating hurricane in the late 1990s leveled many and disfigured others.

Turning onto my father's row, a hush came over us, and we gathered before his cross. Other than our small band, the cemetery was empty.

The personal data on each marker is chiseled into the stone; photographs of the markers do not reveal the wording due to the lack of contrast. Years ago, the American Battle Monuments Commission found a practical solution. The caretaker carries a small pail containing a mud compound, which he spreads onto the marker's face. The dark mud fills the chiseled indentions. When he wipes away the excess mud, the indentions remain filled and the lettering shows up clearly against the white cross.

The sense of communion is so real that I feel I could easily start a conversation with my father. Is this his communion with us? Is the paste the bread? The bucket the chalice? The nearly indistinct letters revealed into the Word? Maybe that's going too far. But my senses heighten and goose bumps form as the attendant wipes the excess mud away, leaving my father's name (my name, my son's name!) visible.

As the attendant backs away, he plants a small American flag, looking both cheap and elegant, into the soft ground at the base of the cross. My son asks him to leave us, as I had done with my mother almost forty years earlier. The attendant withdrew with respect. My son at first kept a distance from the cross, maybe because he had been here before. Or maybe he realized that his name was also on that cross. At twenty-two, he was not ready for the perspective he will one day have. But he will recall his heritage and be thankful.

A flag flies beside the grave of Lt. Conrad John Netting III
in France's Brittany American Cemetery.

We felt the full weight of my father's sacrifice. Most of us cried softly, humbled by his death and victory, by how small we seemed among these heroes.

We forgot to bring flowers. How could we not bring flowers when Normandy had so many rich gardens? I wished we had brought some from the Grandins' garden – to reinforce the link between them and him. My son appeared with some roses from the cemetery's bushes, though this struck me as a meager substitute. Still, he had the right idea, and the hundreds of healthy bushes wouldn't miss the few he had picked.

Forming a rough circle around the cross, we said our prayers, thanking God for the link this trip had provided us and asking Him to continue to care for those, especially my father, who now live with Him. With hoarse voices, we sang the last stanza of *"My Country 'Tis of Thee"* which we sing in our church most Sundays:

> Our fathers' God, to thee, author of liberty, to thee we sing;
> long may our land be bright with freedom's holy light;
> protect us by thy might, great God our King.

We were nearly overwhelmed with emotion at this cemetery, yet we aren't at other grave sites. I can drive by my mother's cemetery a few miles from my home with hardly a thought about her, let alone emotional woolgathering. The difference is that we have so many other connections with my mother and others we were close to; we can remember them in so many settings. We can remember where they taught us, stretched us, energized us, and loved us. When we follow where they led, we feel in contact with them and blessed by them. But we have no such links to my father, other than letters and a few precious treasures. So this simple but powerful gravesite is our key connection and it is where we must come to sense who he was.

Cynthia captured it best. "When we got to Granddad's grave and the family gathered around to pray . . . I began to cry. It was much like what Dad had described about how Momo [Katherine] 'lost it' when she finally went in 1963. Dad said it was like she was finally having a funeral for him. It felt the same for us. Except we were meeting him and saying goodbye at the same moment rather than the others we have known and then lost." Pauleen said: "It was our first time to 'meet' my father-in-law. We were there simply to be with him and remember and connect. To try to feel some of what he must have felt. Then, right away we had to say goodbye. The loss is deep."

Lesley had similar thoughts: "I didn't know what to expect. I never knew this man, yet there was a link. Cross after cross after cross. I imagine them all there in spirit having a party, and I feel a part of it. This is such a beautiful place for him but so far from home. I didn't expect to be so emotional. I felt the need to hug him. But I hugged Dad instead. We said our introductions, then we said our goodbyes."

Jason said: "Nothing can prepare you for this. This made it all too real."

After hugs and tears, we looked at the other markers. How can they be so cold and silent — native white granite has those qualities – yet so warm and telling? We read the chiseled names, units, states of birth, and dates of death and imagined what history each cross or star protects. Each man was an ordinary citizen called to extraordinary duty and sacrifice.

I wondered if each marker and the body it guards had been visited. Who will remember? The parents of these men are gone now, leaving spouses and siblings in their own generation to mourn. The children of the dead, like me, are not young and may not visit that much. When will the visits trail off? When do those who never knew them become the only visitors? Christopher Scanlan wrote of that. He quotes a farmer who lived adjacent to the cemetery: "The young have forgotten all this. . . . That the young who died delivered us. The young – *they* should come here." If they forget or can't be bothered, then the deaths of my father and others who died in the war will become trivialized. I support Les Fleurs de la Mémoire Association in its attempts to encourage the living to honor the dead.

We murmured reluctant good-byes to my father. Then, as we threaded our way through the adjacent markers, we discovered more than a few with unidentified remains. Their crosses spoke poignantly: "Here rests in honored glory a Comrade in Arms known only to God." Farther on, we saw the crosses for twenty pairs of brothers buried side by side, and we thought of the immeasurable grief their parents had endured.

On the graceful curving walls of the central terrace are 498 names of those whose bodies were never recovered, out of about 78,000 worldwide still listed as missing in action. Their inscription reads: "Here are recorded the names of Americans who gave their lives in the service of their country and who sleep in unknown graves. 1941–1945." More despair for more families.

Yet another type of burial is evident. In many cases two men died so violently and in such close proximity that the graves registration detail could not separate their remains. Rather than chance that even a portion of a body be buried under the wrong name, the remains were left inexorably bound together. One cross representing the two men contains both names.

We quickly visited the cemetery's chapel, a cold, gray stone building that seemed out of place among the pristine markers and verdant grass. Though it is supposed to be typically Norman, I've not seen anything like it in the area and I've never liked its look. Adding to its passionless feel is its limited purpose as a place to contemplate the end of life. John Godfrey wrote, "As a house of God it lacked the spiritual feeling of churches I was used to. It was not a church of life, where marriages and baptisms were blessed when people started out on their new lives; here only the end of life was blessed."

Despite the coldness, I was warmed by the prayers from *The Book of Common Prayer* inscribed on the chapel walls:

> O God, who art the author of peace and lover of concord, defend us thy humble servants in all assaults of our enemies, that we surely trusting in thy defense may not fear the power of any adversaries.
>
> O Lord, support us all the day long until the shadows lengthen and our work is done. Then, in thy mercy, grant us a safe lodging and peace at the last.

Though I had those memorized prayers, and recited them hundreds of times, I had never thought of them in the context of my father's death. I would never say them again without thinking of him.

Leaving the cemetery was distressing. I wondered if I would ever be back, if I was leaving without proper homage. If my father in his last year of life had been here with us, he, at twenty-six years old, would be between my children's ages, twenty-two to thirty-two. As Russell Baker wrote in *Good Times,*

> I realized that if my father were mysteriously compelled to join us this day, he would gravitate naturally to my children for companionship. If he noticed me staring curiously at him, he might turn . . . and whisper, asking, 'Who's the old man in the high-priced suit?' I was old enough to be his father.
>
> So it is with a family. We carry the dead generations within us and pass them on to the future aboard our children. This keeps the people of the past alive long after we have taken them to the churchyard.

———————— ✶ ————————

CHAPTER EIGHTEEN

A New Monument in Saint-Michel-des-Andaines

Saint-Michel-des-Andaines, the village where my father died, fulfilled my notion of what a Normandy village should be. Set in a wide, shallow valley, its skyline consisted of one feature, the church's steeple. Sprinkled around in all directions were pale rooftops between the trees. Two narrow roads intersected near the church, with cars giving the only evidence of the twenty-first, or even the twentieth, century.

We had dashed from St. James cemetery to our hotel for a quick change of clothes, then from the hotel to Saint-Michel-des-Andaines. We allowed fifteen minutes to get to the site of the dedication, but it took less than five. Since no one was at the site, we drove a short distance away, killed the engine, and waited in thought.

So much had led us to this tiny bit of a town, none of it instigated by me. Without exception others had done all the work. My father had been the hero, my mother had packed the footlocker, Louis Grandin had defied authority, and Michel Grandin had done research beyond what even the most dedicated Netting family member would have done. And all of it had been handed to me. My effort, other than to follow through, had been slight at best: arrange to open the footlockers, schedule a trip or two, and conduct a few interviews. Reactive steps.

Why was I the blessed recipient? It haunts me to think that I didn't begin my own research in my twenties, or at least before a French family had to do it for me. Was I that busy? Was I without enough sense of place to wonder what happened after the crash? Apparently so. Even with increasingly provocative segments of the story revealed to me, I did little additional research. Emotionally exhausted, I was embarrassed that I had done so little but grateful that so many had done so much. I recalled Psalm 32:14: I trust in you, O Lord, saying, "You are my God!" My future is in your hands.

I started the car and turned toward the village

Though we were within a few minutes of 2:30 p.m., the Normans, true to Gallic custom, were not in sight. We parked on the gravel road just off the blacktop that connects Saint-Michel-des-Andaines with La Ferté-Macé. The Saint-Michel-des-Andaines cemetery sits at the intersection of those two roads about half a kilometer from where we had surveyed the town with the journalists. The side road is extra wide for the first 100 meters, which allows for a few cars to park head-in at the cemetery wall. We had read that the town council picked that wall for the memorial because it was close to where my father destroyed the German trucks and near where he lay buried for several months.

I noticed an indeterminate form beside the wall, about three feet square and covered in red, white, and blue bunting. In front of that was a carefully cultivated bed of flowers, all freshly planted for the summer. This must be the memorial.

Within minutes others arrived, including the mayor, official looking in his French tricolor sash; the deputy mayor; and other dignitaries. Close behind them were the Grandins and eventually many of the townspeople. We later learned that at least 135 attended from a village of about 300. My impressions were that this small town had not changed much over the decades, either in sophistication or inhabitants. Everyone I spoke with was genuine, grateful for a break in the routine, and, to my mind, still somewhat in awe of my father and his heroism.

As we ambled about, I noticed an elderly gentleman unfurl three flags, one U.S. flag and two French flags, with considerable care. He placed them above the memorial, with the American flag higher than the other two. I tensed and waited for someone to correct the placement so the French flag would be higher. But no one corrected him and no one would, because that is the honor they pay Americans in this part of France. Eventually someone called for order and the ceremony began.

As with most civic functions, there is a hierarchy to be observed. Someone introduced the mayor, small and well into his seventies, who, positioned behind a portable podium, welcomed the guests and the townspeople. He introduced Jacques Pottier, a man of perhaps fifty-five, lean and ruddy. He had spent months searching for records and making contacts.

I didn't follow what they were saying in French, but a new interpreter, assigned to me, motioned for my son and me to step up to the cemetery wall, between the podium and the bunting, above which were now flying the three flags. The interpreter had no chance to do her job, since to translate a speech on the fly was almost impossible. She gave up and I understood why.

Soon my son and I were guided to the plaque and, through my interpreter, asked to remove the bunting. We at last saw the result of the villagers' efforts. First I noticed a large stone slab maybe four feet tall and three feet wide, irregularly shaped. Affixed to its center was a bronze plaque of about fifteen by twenty inches. A full-color patch of the Eighth Air Force anchored the upper left corner. In the upper right corner was an American flag in red, white, and blue. Below them was this inscription:

A la mémoire du Lt. NETTING Conrad J.
8th U. S. Air Force No. 0694174
Mort pour la liberté
Le 10/6/1944
Repose a St-James E.13.5

It was perfection. I wouldn't have changed a letter on it. The colors, the wording (in French, but easily translated), the positioning, everything was perfect. Even the flowers growing at the base were exactly right. I knew Michel Grandin would make sure they were tended properly. The people of Saint-Michel-des-Andaines and their town council did a fine job. Even the location was ideal – near the crash site, near my father's first burial site, near the graves of Louis and Marie-Louise Grandin and Abbé Eugène Hochet, the priest.

Lesley said later: "The memorial is beautiful. I think it is perfect to be next to the cemetery that Mr. Grandin's parents are buried in. I like it that [the memorial] is alone, not with any other. Makes Granddad stand out even more."

William Hazlitt, the essayist, wrote, "Those only deserve a monument who do not need one." That was never more true to my mind than for this hero.

At the dedication of the monument at Saint-Michel-des-Andaines to Lieutenant Netting are, from left, Mayor Raymond Gérault, Conrad John Netting IV, Michel Grandin and archivist Jacques Pottier.

A la mémoire du Lt NETTING CONRAD.J.
8 th U.S. AIR FORCE N°0694174
Mort pour la liberté
Le 10.6.1944
Repose à St-James E.13.5

Tears filled my eyes again. Warm applause from the crowd followed the unveiling. After admiring the plaque we returned to our places.

The deputy mayor continued in French, presumably welcoming us to the ceremony. After a few minutes, he stopped, the crowd seemed to catch its breath, and I heard a few scratches over the portable public address system, followed by the pop-pop-pop of a well-used record. I was astonished to hear "The Star-Spangled Banner." In the middle of France! With the American flag waving gently, almost in rhythm, just a dozen feet from me. I felt my jaw drop, though the photos say it didn't. The feeling was there. I recovered my composure and placed my hand over my heart, hoping my son had done the same. He had. And Jake, in his Class A, U.S. Army uniform, snapped to attention and rendered a crisp salute. My son later commented how the wind played with the flag and that the dense green hedge, almost five feet tall, was the perfect backdrop for the memorial.

Later, comparing notes with my family, I learned that they and the villagers had also been overwhelmed. The crowd audibly caught its breath when the music started, resulting in tissues and handker-chiefs dabbed at the eyes. Cynthia wrote: "So often Americans hear this anthem and simply go through the motions. On that day we went through emotions. The song seemed so powerful and true and touch-ing. I am more proud than ever to be an American and free. In World War II we fought and Granddad died so that others might be allowed to get a small glimpse of that freedom."

Jason wrote: "On this day 'The Star-Spangled Banner' was extra special. I felt deep pride seeing Conrads IV and V facing the American flag and Jake Stewart in uniform saluting." And Pauleen wrote: "I will never forget the moment the 'The Star-Spangled Banner' was played. Everyone was moved. Tears on every cheek. Jake, being in uniform, was a special treat and a reminder of what American soldiers stand for. You are just overwhelmed by how much thoughtfulness and respect the Normans have for the Americans who fought, and for us, their family members."

The longer we were in France, and especially Normandy, the more we saw the American flag both in public settings – squares, memorials, and roundabouts – and on small homes and modest shops. Though we were there just after D-Day, it was still obvious that the Normans remember those who helped set them free.

The deputy mayor began the formal part of his presentation. Fortunately, a written translation meant we could follow along.

> We are gathered together today to commemorate an event which took place fifty-eight years ago in our village. St.-Michel has not forgotten the man every-one called "the American pilot."

On behalf of the local population and our Mayor, I have been asked to tell you, Mr. Netting, and your relatives as well, how sincerely we share your emotion and your sorrow, too, at the very place where a cruel war made an orphan of you even before you were born.

He continued in his rhythmic French to bring to mind the events of "that painful event" on June 10 and 11, 1944. After he recalled the burial and the "mountain of flowers," he said, "Mr. Netting, we can assure you that the local population paid to your father the homage due to him. Far away from his family and native country, he could then rest in peace." Indeed he could. "As you can see," he said, sweeping his hand toward the crowd, "the people of St. Michel have not forgotten their American pilot." He continued,

May I tell you again how affectionate the French people are toward the American people? At decisive moments in history, our two countries have been side by side in the fight for freedom.

Thanks to the kind collaboration of Intendant Jacques Adelée of St. James Cemetery, recent new research enabled us to discover the true identity of Lieutenant Netting. In 2001, the local council decided to have a commemorative plaque made and asked the Méllanger Company to furnish the plaque. At that time we could not have imagined seeing the Netting family here.

We want these moving moments we are relating now to be engraved in our memories as a testimony to peace. And may Lieutenant Netting, who made a gift of his life, serve as an example to future generations.

The attentive crowd struggled to hold back tears. Jason said: "You could see it in their eyes and through their reactions that they did not just stop by to see what was going on. Each one had some personal tie to this event fifty-eight years ago. Plus, you knew that these people realized what this meant to Conrad IV and his family. There was a deep sense of respect and appreciation."

✻ ✻ ✻

I was flattered and humbled that the mayor and deputy mayor had spoken so eloquently. But since the events took place in their town they were almost required to attend. I was thinking too small. Next to speak was the congressman from the Saint-Michel-des-Andaines district, who had made the five-hour drive from Paris for the occasion. His presence was further evidence that the events of June 1944 were of highest importance to the Normans.

He began his comments in French, and without notes, so at first I couldn't understand him. But after a few minutes, he continued in English and became noticeably emotional. His remarks were compelling.

> It's an honor and a pleasure to have you here today and, as you know, here in Normandy we'll never forget the American blood spread on our beaches and on our soil. We think of you, we stand by you. Every time liberty is in danger, France and the United States are on the same side. Of course, I'm thinking of what happened on September 11, too. God bless your family. God bless the families of all those who died for our freedom. God bless America.

I was surprised at his candor and his overt alliance with the United States. But I shouldn't have been, because despite my sense that France has not always been an ally of the United States recently, he represents an area of France that is consistently loyal to America.

Pauleen later wrote: "The congressman's speech was powerful – I felt he truly meant what he said. This is another example of how our family's story touches everyone." My son wrote, "There were tears in the congressman's eyes. The crowd, teary also, nodded in agreement."

After the congressman finished to enthusiastic applause, the deputy mayor motioned for me to make my comments. I was eager to offer my affirmation of the theme of liberty. I had planned what I might say and written down the highlights. But language was again an issue. My translator and I had to share the microphone, which was awkward, so I trimmed wherever possible:

> Thank you for the honor you paid my family and me today. We are grateful to you, to Les Fleurs de la Mémoire Association, and especially to the Grandin family for their devotion to my father and what he sacrificed. That devotion has stood for fifty-eight years.
>
> But today we celebrate more than one life and more than one battle; we celebrate freedom. My father wanted a big family, four or five boys, and a ranch in Texas. But that didn't happen. What did happen he could never have foreseen: he helped bring freedom where it wasn't and, along the way, helped win a war.
>
> This one battle that we commemorate today, which is so small compared to the whole of World War II, helped freedom ring, beginning in this village, then throughout this country, and finally throughout the world. We lost him and his dreams, but we gained freedom. Today we remember one from the greatest generation, but let us never forget that there were 330,000 others stationed in England, all willing every day to sacrifice their lives. Such willingness stands fast in the Bible in John 15:13: "Greater love has no man than this, that he would lay down his life for his friends." To his friends who are now our friends, to all of you, thank you.

After my comments the deputy mayor asked anyone who would like to speak to come forward, thus ending the formalities. Two elderly ladies, short, dressed in their Sunday best, and with cheeks the color of Normandy apples, came up. Despite the language barrier, I gleaned one fact: they, too, were witnesses to the crash and explosion. They had harbored those events and now sought to claim a link to my father's life through me. I was struck at how routine this seemed to everyone, almost an afterthought.

These ladies were two of several there who saw the crash. To tell their stories was no big deal to them, though they told them with obvious emotion. I was incredulous to have these links to my father. I didn't have enough time to talk with them, and my translators were helping my family, so I smiled sheepishly and thanked them.

Cynthia wrote: "I cannot imagine what it was like for the French to have war in their backyards. I am so glad the United States did all we could to stop that. God bless America and France and especially the Normans." Pauleen wrote: "I can't imagine what it was like to be occupied by Germans. That is why the older generation of Normandy remembers Conrad III so well, because they lived it. That is obvious all the time we are in the Normandy countryside."

An older gentleman got the interpreter's attention and began telling her a long story. She relayed to me that his father had owned the farm on which my father's plane crashed, that he and Michel Grandin were friends and that he had also seen the crash. Though he had since sold the farm, he had visited the crash site a few months earlier and had, after superficial digging, found a piece of the plane's wreckage. He ceremoniously handed it to me. Part of me was delighted to hold this palm-sized piece of the plane my father had named for me. Another part was unnerved that I held something that could easily have had my father's blood on it. I soldiered on, expressing my thanks, and hoped my expression was properly interpreted. The crowd applauded.

He then invited me to tour the crash site with him. That caused me more concern, but I said I would. Sylvie, who overheard this, said it would have to wait.

After the remaining impromptu speeches, the crowd, which had been a respectful distance away in a semicircle, came forth to greet one another and us. Several asked for my autograph, including the two ladies who had seen the crash. I remembered reading that for autographs you should ask for a name and personalize your message. When I asked for names, I got puzzled looks. Once again my lack of French was an issue. I settled on "To my friend" instead. I was not the hero nor had I seen the hero, but still I represent the hero. I sensed they'd just transferred their awe over these events to me, and that felt odd. Yet I provided the closure the village needed. And that's okay.

As conversations were winding down, Sylvie said it was time for the reception. I remembered hearing about a reception earlier, but I thought this was it. But the town was sponsoring a gathering with refreshments at the town hall. Just before we left, Jake noticed the Grandins retiring the colors, French and American. Later, he wrote: "The Colors. Carefully, deliberately, affectionately . . . they retire the colors. Paying tribute to a man and a nation with seasoned hands and dignified movement. Like the strokes of an impressionist painter, each turn of the flag carries genuine expression and meaning. And so, with an Honor Guard present, this French couple offers quiet closure . . . Sharing a glimpse of the colors that a Human Spirit can hold."

* * *

In Saint-Michel-des-Andaines, like most small towns, residents measure variety by the weather. When any chance for more substantial change comes, most will seize it. This Norman village's headquarters, a solid two story building, perhaps the largest in town after the church, seemed to shine in the unfettered sunlight. The main room was big enough to hold half the town, as it did that day. Along one side was a table full of wine glasses and trays of cookies. The cookies were tasty, but the French champagne was delicious.

The thinning ranks at the memorial did not suggest lack of interest. The assembly had only migrated to this place. The reverberating conversations made normal talking impossible, but that stopped no one. A man introduced himself as Stéphane Robine, the public archivist in Flers, a small town twenty-six kilometers away. After barely a hello, Stéphane, who spoke first-rate English, showed me a page with information about my father, his Missing Air Crew Report. I didn't know what surprised me more, that this young man, probably not yet thirty, was, like the Grandins, doing research on my father, or that there was more new data. Either would have been surprising, both were bewildering.

I also spoke with Jacques Adelée, an American and the chief caretaker of the Brittany American Cemetery at St. James, an amiable man who looks the part in his black uniform with gold buttons. I noticed him at the ceremony but could not place the uniform or his role.

He told me it was the uniform of the American Battle Monuments Commission, the agency that manages American cemeteries and other sites in America and overseas. His dramatic silver hair and mustache, tall frame, and open expression fit the uniform perfectly. A retired military officer, he has had plenty of practice wearing a uniform. Regrettably, he said, he was not at the cemetery that morning when we visited my father's grave. He expected us to visit but didn't know when.

Managing the cemetery includes inspection of the crosses and stars, and he said he noticed a discoloration in my father's cross, which he would look into. If it is endemic to the granite, a disease, he'll have the cross replaced. I said I was reluctant to change crosses for any reason since my forebears have revered what that cross represents. He said he wouldn't act without telling me, though if the disease in the granite continues to spread, he will have to replace it.

A rich assortment of townspeople made their way over to offer hellos and welcomes through my interpreter, who helped me with these brief conversations. Pauleen observed: "Everyone wanted to talk in French to us. We could not understand, but their eyes said they had been a part of the story and were glad to be there with us and meet the American soldier's family. They had a need to put a face and body and personality to Conrad III, which they could do by meeting us. They offered lots of talk, kisses, hugs, and smiles."

Later I thought of all the books I've read, all the research I've done on World War II, and how the older people who took me into their confidence and told me how their lives briefly touched my father's lived the war under German occupation. The books were second-hand reports. Now I had the genuine article. I was among people who lived the war every day. How extraordinary. I should have had a tape recorder, but I didn't and I'm sorry.

Jason, who noticed Michel talking animatedly with his friends, said: "I remember how Mr. Grandin interacted with the townspeople. Before, he was the shy man who didn't say much, but among his friends and family, he was cheery and social. Although humble, he seemed proud and satisfied with the events of the day. I can still see his smiling face and as with all of his expressions, it spoke volumes."

Later, the farmer came up and began talking again about the events of June 10 and 11, 1944. He was obviously enjoying his notoriety as landowner and archeologist. He repeated many of the facts we had heard from the Grandins, though with a relish that was engaging. And he appeared ready to take us on a tour of the site.

Pauleen said: "The village's reception was a thoughtful gesture. Simple drinks and cookies, perfectly in sync with the village's style. They live a simple but meaningful life. We, as Americans, could learn from that. I felt very loved for being Conrad III's daughter-in-law."

Through some coordination, Sylvie knew it was time to head for the site and shepherded us back to the cars. We pressed on, amazed at our good fortune.

CHAPTER NINETEEN

--- ★ ---

Some Time to Reflect

Back at the Saint-Michel-des-Andaines cemetery, we parked and assembled for the short walk to the site of my father's crash. About one-fourth of the villagers at the ceremony had returned. The farmer took the lead down a one-lane dirt road that passed a farmhouse and assorted barns and sheds. The new owner and his son, who was about my age, walked with me, though the language barrier precluded any conversation. All three farmers seemed proud that this land was the center of so much attention.

The road soon ended. We stepped carefully around the muddy yard and avoided the rusting farm implements. Behind the last building was a small ravine that we crossed with the help of some boards Michel found for us to walk on. Then we were in the Andaines forest. The undergrowth is lime green and perhaps knee-high. But everyone trooped on through the remaining fifty meters, even the ladies in their skirts and stockings. Though the day was warm and bright, in the forest we felt the damp, cool air and could smell the sweet odor of undisturbed leaves and lush growth.

Fifty-eight years and several hurricanes later, the crash site was hardly distinguished. Jason wrote: "There was no real evidence of what happened there nearly sixty years ago. Trees and groundcover had grown over the site, so we just examined an indentation or crevice in the landscape. Was this from the impact of the crash or just the natural terrain?"

We learned from the previous owner that it was the natural terrain. The forest consisted of trees that reached skyward maybe 100 meters with almost no lower branches. The crash site, however, was at the edge of a clearing in the trees, suggesting that maybe the explosion had cleared this space. The farmer said it did not, and if it had, new growth would have replaced it.

From this site, we were told, the original owner dug up the plane part he presented to me at the dedication. I was then, and am even more so now, at a loss for how to react. My instinct told me this was macabre, that the piece was twisted and misshapen, giving evidence of pain and torment. I learned that the elderly farmer found this piece after just an hour or two of digging a few months before our arrival. I tried to sort through my feelings.

I wasn't the only one. Several times I noticed Conrad V off by himself, apparently deep in thought. He looked down, then up, then off at the distant tree line. What was he thinking? He could be thinking about the unnaturalness of visiting a death site. Or he could be coming to grips with how unique these events were. Or he could be contemplating how his descendants might some day figure in this story. Would he bring them here in twenty years? How will he and his sisters pass on to their children and grandchildren the legacy of this family? How will that help them define what they are made of? Plenty to think about, apart in the trees of the Andaines forest.

A half-hour after we arrived, our band of twenty or thirty began our walk back to the cemetery. Small talk emanated from clusters of two and three, but generally the mood was quiet. I walked in silence with Mr. Grandin. I sensed that he and I didn't need to talk just now. Family came to my mind, and I thought of him as a long-lost relative with whom I needed to spend a little more time catching up.

As we gathered by the cars, only the Grandin family, about a dozen, and our family of seven remained. I suggested a walk through the Saint-Michel-des-Andaines cemetery, maybe fifty meters square, to see the first burial place of my father. Pictures I had seen showed the gravesite unused, but I assumed that over the years someone else had been buried there. Not so. The site was still empty. Surely someone owned this plot, but if so they were not in a rush to use it. Another memorial, in a sense, to their venerated American pilot.

A few steps away were the graves of Louis and Marie-Louise Grandin and Abbé Hochet, all players in the drama. No doubt some day the cemetery will hold the bodies of Michel and Louisette Grandin. Pauleen said: "I'm happy to see how close the Grandins and the priest's graves are to Conrad III's first grave. They were all simple, honest, good people. They should be together. They thought of others first."

Jason wrote: "It was satisfying to see the Grandin family's resting place in the cemetery and only fitting that the man who helped bury Conrad III would be buried just 50 yards or so from his memorial and 150 yards from the crash site. Conrads IV and V will always be able to pay their respects to the Grandin family at the same time they visit the memorial."

Lesley added: "Going to the cemetery closed the circle. I couldn't help but feel the need to say 'thank you' to Mr. Grandin Sr. I felt like Granddad was there, as though his resting place was there and not at the Brittany Cemetery. I liked the thought of Granddad being close to the senior Grandins, as if they are still watching over him, still taking care of him."

As we walked, our footsteps crunching on the gravel walkways, Michel, through Sylvie's translation, pointed to a cross about eight feet tall over a gravesite near the roadway. The bottom corner of the horizontal arm is missing its filigree. Michel explained that this ornamentation was shot off by my father's machine guns during the strafing attack. He said this with an impish grin, suggesting it might be more town lore than historical fact. But I didn't ask for proof one way or the other.

As a Christian, I was especially pleased that my father's first burial place was adjacent to the base of a tall stone cross reaching perhaps fifteen meters toward the heavens. This cross, standing like a lighthouse, sends signals of hope, compassion, understanding, and redemption to all who would believe. What a perfect symbol to stand watch over the battle site, the crash site, the graves, and the town. Within a tight radius from that cross was a grave or memorial of all the players in the story and, some day, maybe the graves of those who saw the crash and have remembered it so well today.

Two sons, two fathers, one story. All monitored by the dramatic cross representing another Son and Father.

By now we had been on our feet for over three hours, and weariness suddenly overcame us. We said our goodbyes to the Grandins but made one more appointment, a meal together the following evening.

On that Sunday, our last day in Normandy, we had dinner in the small dining room of our inn. Because of the newspaper articles and the television show, we had become minor celebrities, and the hotel staff did all they could to make our last evening flawless. The meal – in true French tradition – lasted several hours. The hotel kept adding lagniappes, resulting in, we think, eleven courses total. Despite all that, the food was secondary. The best course was the friendship we had developed with our new extended family – the Grandins and Christiane Gillette. Pauleen wrote:

> Our last meal with the Grandins and Mrs. Gillette was perfect: the food, the feeling of knowing each other, and of knowing we will miss each other. I feel they are now a part of our family, they are just in France. Mrs. Gillette, too! I wished the evening did not have to end.
>
> I want to remember Conrad III, the people of Normandy (both during the war and now), and all the experiences we had. I want to be that type of person: caring, giving, knowing my duty and following through. They knew honor, respect, and history. They were thoughtful, genuine, quiet, and so much more.

We said *au revoir* that evening, with every intention to keep our new friendships alive over the coming years. And we will. A few months after our trip, Michel and Louisette wrote us, "Those few days lived together were full of emotion [and] gratitude to your father and to his ultimate sacrifice, and to my own father for the dignity and the nobleness of his soul." Amen.

Jason said, "A common bond from an event fifty-eight years ago brought our families together, but it's the warm and kind generosity and fellowship we shared that promises to hold this relationship together for many years." We will know them better, and they us.

Lesley wrote, "They have become like grandparents to me. I had no idea how much that space needed to be filled. When your grandparents have been gone so long you remember how much you loved them but forget how much you need them."

* * *

Knowing how my father died and how the Normans tenderly took care of his body brings my father's life story to a close for me. Knowing that my mother, grandparents, and uncles all died without this healing news still hurts. But wouldn't they know all this in heaven? Maybe they have hurt for me, until now. Maybe they, now joined with him, are smiling.

Afterword

A substory to this book is how coincidences serendipitously led us to learn a legacy so long delayed. The footlocker and the package from France were two major links in that story's chain. A more recent event was less significant but equally dramatic.

In April 2005, after my manuscript had gone to the publisher, I was introduced to a lady at a small party. She said she had heard my family's name a few days earlier in connection with the couple who bought the house my mother had lived in with her second husband for twenty years. The couple had found a large box of Netting family documents that was out of sight when my stepfather's estate sold the house, more than ten years after my mother's death.

Two days after hearing this news, I visited the couple and was given the box. They had held it for almost two years, wondering what to do with it. I inventoried the contents, which ranged in date from 1915 to 1962. Many items were incidental and not worth keeping for so long.

Others were invaluable: the first letter my father wrote to my mother (1941); the letters from Pat Patteeuw to my mother (1944–45); the remembrance of my mother receiving the first telegram; and, most importantly, the telegrams reporting that my father was missing and that he had been killed. Fortunately, I was still able to integrate the new material into this book.

I have no idea why these precious artifacts were not in the foot-locker. If my mother took them on purpose to her new home in 1974, why such a variety of documents that cover so many years? And why didn't she mention them to me? I'll ask her those questions some day.

This story is applicable to every family in every war. The difference is that the full story has been revealed to us, while your story, perhaps, may still be shrouded in bureaucracy or sealed in a dusty footlocker. Someday you may uncover your story, or you may not. No matter. The point is that your story has just as good a chance as mine to have happened, and you should take comfort in that.

The American World War II Orphans Network (AWON), a non-profit organization that serves as a clearinghouse for those who lost a father during World War II, reports that there might have been 183,000 such orphans, a staggering number. The founder of AWON, Ann Bennett Mix, wrote in *Lost in the Victory*:

> We struggled against our mothers' desire to forget and our own desire to remember. While many mothers needed to forget that painful episode in their young lives, we – the orphans – needed to know about our fathers. We are now in our fifties. We have completed our educations, raised our families, and established our careers.
>
> Now it is as if we are awakening from a dream in which our fathers were lost to us. We want to know who they were. Perhaps our awakening is occurring as we begin to face our own mortality and think about the linkage of our lives, the past and the future. We are beginning to ask the unanswered questions: How and where did our fathers die? Is there anyone who was with them when they died? Are there those who remember them? Are there pictures or letters to provide clues that can help us know our fathers?
>
> We are beginning to find the answers. We are beginning to realize how profoundly our lives have been affected by our losses. We want our children to know their grandfathers. We want to learn all we can before it is too late.

The reality is that, until God had us open that footlocker, I knew my father partly through a sepia-toned portrait of a young man in uniform and partly through remnants of long-ago conversations. Now I see him clearly, more so perhaps than many whose fathers returned – or never left.

Even if your father or other relative returned but wouldn't speak of the war, he might have had such heroic experiences. If so, maybe he's ready to talk, to let the sometimes terrible stories be heard. Many men left the war behind decades ago, forging a truce with the truth. But time and their mortality are bringing their experiences to the surface, where they can deposit them into their families' verbal scrapbooks.

And what of those men – and women – in supporting roles? George H. W. Bush said, "Any definition of a successful life must include service to others." He doesn't specify where that service must take place. Their stories are just as important as those from the edge of battle.

My experience has been that the war's veterans are becoming more willing to speak than they were when first we labeled them "the silent generation." The passing years have probably encouraged their disclosures. If a veteran lives in your family, begin your research right away. I interviewed Pat Patteeuw, my father's wingman, in 1997 and garnered hours of audiotape with his lucid recollections. Five years later I learned he had Alzheimer's disease. One year after that, he died.

Your family's story may be incomplete for extraneous reasons. In fact, 78,000 Americans who fought in World War II are still listed as missing. If so, you can – you must – learn more, for your satisfaction and for the future generations in your family who will someday want to know but who will have far more difficulty with the research. You'll find some helpful support in the resources section of this book.

On the fiftieth anniversary of D-Day, the Rev. Ted Schroder, rector of my Episcopal church, said in his sermon, "What do these true heroes have to teach us today? That victory over evil is going to cost us something dear, that we have to be willing to sacrifice for the things that are worthwhile, that we must be prepared to do what is needed in order to make progress, to protect our friends, to attain our objectives." Each generation must step forward – whether in Korea, Vietnam, or Iraq – to defend its freedom, thus ensuring its own greatness. The heroes keep coming, giving truth to the words of Thomas Paine: "If there must be trouble, let it be in my day, so that my children may have peace."

I have been blessed beyond all reasonable expectation to learn my family's story, and to learn it the way I did. Yours may be waiting for you. Why not start your research today?

To help you learn more about your family's role in World War II, here are some resources that might prove helpful. Internet sites were current at the date of publication. You might find additional help by using books and publications mentioned in the index. Each resource has additional material and links that can further your research.

American Air Museum and Imperial War Museum Duxford, www.iwm.org.uk/duxford/

American Battle Monuments Commission, www.abmc.gov

American World War II Orphans Network (AWON), www.awon.org

Association of the Fourth Fighter Group, 1077 Clipper Mill Drive, West Chester, PA 19382-5292

Cost of Freedom, www.costoffreedom.org

D-Day Museum, www.ddaymuseum.org

Duxford Museum, www.iwm.org.uk/duxford/

East of England Tourist Board, www.visiteastofengland.com

Eighth Air Force Historical Society, www.8thafhs.org

4th Fighter Group, www.fourthfightergroup.com

The Legacy Project, www.warletters.com

Les Fleurs de la Mémoire Association, http://fleursdelamemoire.free.fr

Little Friends, www.littlefriends.co.uk

Mighty 8th Air Force Museum, www.mightyeighth.org

ACKNOWLEDGMENTS

Just as my father was surrounded by support as he sought to complete his missions, so was I as I wrote this book. To thank everyone who helped me – family, friends, coworkers, and proofreaders – would require another book. To them I offer public thanks for your patience and encouragement.

Several supporters must be named, however, as their help went beyond reasonable bounds. To two French villages, La Ferté-Macé and Saint-Michel-des-Andaines, thank you for being so warm, welcoming, and wonderful. To Betsy Wray and Janet Payne, thank you for your quiet retreats where nearly all of the manuscript was created. To Andy Carroll, thank you for absorbing the most poignant of my mother's writings into *Behind the Lines,* and for the foreword to this book. To Sue Turner, thank you for your up-close introduction to the American Battle Monuments Commission. To Phillip Bagnal, thank you for believing in the project almost before it existed. To USAA and Lisa Severson, thank you for printing excerpts for USAA members. To my children, Lesley, Cynthia, and Conrad V, thank you for the future generations in whom this story will, with your guidance, be instilled.

This book would not exist except for the perseverance and determination of a gentle French family who fought bureaucracy and repeated setbacks but would not give up their dream. Would that we all had their passion for answers to lingering questions. To the Nettings' adopted French family, Michel, Louisette, and Sylvie, thank you for finding us.

As I struggled with the beginnings of this book, I learned the value of a muse, defined as a spirit that inspires a writer. As the manuscript evolved, my spiritual muse was often absent without leave. Blessedly, my physical muse was ever present, always supportive, never compromising, and fully involved. I cannot thank her enough for the inspiration she was to this book. To Pauleen, I love you.

INDEX

Stewart, Cynthia Netting (Mrs. Jake), 141, 155, 164, 189, 193
Stewart, Jake, 189, 193
Tallahassee, Florida, 46–47
Texas A&M University, 12–13, 28–29, 141, 155
Toutain, Françis, 121, 122
Trenton, Michigan, 13
U.S. Army Air Corps, 26–27, 33, 36–37, 39; Eighth Air Force 59, 107, 187; 4th Fighter Group, 56, 59–60, 78, 79, 81, 107, 207; 54th Fighter Group, 47; 496th Fighter Group, 53
U.S. Army Air Corps aircraft, B-17 Fortress, 64; B-24 Liberator, 64; P-47 Thunderbolt, 60; P-51 Mustang, 60–64, 75, 82
U.S. Army Corps of Engineers, 24
Uvalde, Texas, 36–37
V-Mail, 68–69
World War I, 117–18, 117
World War II, 23–24, 39, 115

Conrad John Netting IV was born in San Antonio one month after his pilot father's death following the 1944 D-Day invasion in World War II. He graduated from Alamo Heights High School and holds degrees from the University of Texas at Austin and Texas A&M University. Netting served stateside during Vietnam as an Army officer at Fort Hood, Texas. He is a partner at Netting & Pace, CPAs. His hobbies include being an avocational historian with a focus on World War I, and he lives in San Antonio.